Triumph of the Light

The Story of Humanity's Enslavement and
Impending Liberation

First Edition Design Publishing
Sarasota, Florida USA

Triumph of the Light
Copyright ©2017 Vidya Frazier

ISBN 978-1506-905-17-4 PRINT
ISBN 978-1506-905-18-1 EBOOK

LCCN 20179599530

November 2017

Published and Distributed by
First Edition Design Publishing, Inc.
P.O. Box 20217, Sarasota, FL 34276-3217
www.firsteditiondesignpublishing.com

Triumph of the Light

The Story of Humanity's Enslavement and Impending Liberation

Vidya Frazier

Contents

Preface

This is a book I never imagined I would be writing. In the past, my writing has always focused on the process of individual awakening or "ascension" – the very personal experience of passing through these times of great transformation as an individual. It has been my passion and joy to help guide people through the often tricky and sometimes frightening passageways of the awakening process that is occurring within so many in the world at this time.

So it came as a great surprise to me when I awoke one morning with the knowing that it was now time for me to turn toward the phenomenon of the collective ascension of the human race and to begin writing about that.

It's not as if I had been unaware of the larger picture of the shift humanity as a whole is making into a freer and more expansive consciousness that has been called the "Fifth Dimension". Indeed, I had been very aware of it as the "back-drop" of the individual process of ascension I was writing about. And I'd also had numerous profound heart-opening experiences in which my love for humanity as a whole would just flood me, bringing on tears of compassion and grief for the seemingly senseless suffering this collective has endured for so long.

However, I tended to keep some distance from the larger picture as it was playing out in the world of geopolitical events, seeing this current global situation to be both transitory and chaotic, and thus something I'd preferably not want to get caught up in.

But then, at some point I found myself reading more and more about all the exciting and sometimes disquieting information that was being disclosed on alternative internet sites. Whistle-blowers from many of the intelligence agencies and the military were suddenly coming out of the woodwork disclosing a huge variety of previously hidden information and nefarious goings-on behind the scenes in secret space projects, secret societies, and elite-infested corporations. It was both fascinating and disturbing to read the reports of those who had been on the inside of these stories.

Yet still, I had never thought I would be one to help guide others to all this information – until a sense of urgency about doing just that suddenly arose, and writing began flowing out of me at a pace I could barely keep up with.

My aim with this book has been to try to capture all the many different facets of disclosure that are now occurring with increasing speed and depth. I have aimed to simply introduce and highlight as many different aspects of the disclosures as I can and then give references for further research for those interested in pursuing the information.

I have also attempted to present all the disclosures in as positive a light as possible, so as to bring a sense of empowerment and optimism to the reader. And, very importantly, I have emphasized that all of the corruption and control that is being revealed is now finally being addressed, as people awaken and respond to it with conscious practices and activism – and also as what's been called the "Light Forces" work to help eliminate it all from the planet.

I am aware that some of the information I present is not new to many informed readers. I don't imagine it would be a surprise for most people reading this book that we are living with institutions, especially in the West, that are deeply flawed and corrupt. Most are also aware, at least to some degree, of the small elite group of people known as the "Cabal" or the "Illuminati", who essentially run the world's financial, military, religious and geopolitical institutions.

However, I have found that many people tend to be unaware of the actual depth and scope of the corruption that reigns – and, in many ways, actually enslaves us. And most are totally unaware of the dark extra-terrestrial manipulation that has actually lain behind the Cabal's control of the planet.

I believe that for us to wake up and fully shift into a liberated fifth-dimensional consciousness, we need to attend to more than our own personal awakening. We need also to become aware of ourselves as participants in the human collective and how we must, as an entire group, break free of the control and manipulation that we have suffered from for eons of time. Only then will we make a collective leap as a species into an expansive new consciousness of freedom and empowerment.

Hopefully this book will help you to make that leap yourself; and in the process, perhaps help you to assist others to make it as well.

Vidya Frazier,
November 2017

Chapter 1

The Global Shift

There's no doubt about it. The world looks absolutely crazy these days. According to most news sources, chaos and conflict are raging across the planet, and events seem to be spiraling out of control. It can be downright scary to take it all in.

It's also difficult to even know what to believe anymore about what's actually occurring in the world. With all the "fake news" in both the mainstream media and the alternative internet media, it's nearly impossible to be certain about what is really happening – or about how any of it may impact our personal lives.

In looking at it all, you can't help but wonder: Is humanity finally on its way to extinction?

A Leap in Evolution

I invite you to consider the possibility that something else very different is happening: that all the chaos occurring now in the world may actually be a sign that humanity is currently in the process of preparing for a huge leap in evolution. And that what we are now witnessing is simply a very messy and chaotic transitional phase taking place within that enormous shift.

This shift has actually been predicted for centuries – and even for thousands of years, in some cases – by visionaries, prophets and indigenous elders across the globe, and it has also been described in a wide variety of ancient spiritual texts and depicted on historic artifacts.

There are even certain scientists who have described these times as a natural phase that occurs within the evolution of a species. And others who indicate that the earth is currently traveling through a part of the galaxy it passes through every 26,000 years or so; and that during these previous times the earth has been in this position, the human race has passed through chaotic times that eventually resolved into what have been described as "Golden Ages". Within this part of the galaxy – the middle of the Milky Way – there evidently exist certain cosmic phenomena and frequencies that help to ignite this evolutionary process.

In recent years, people have named this current shift in human consciousness simply as the "Shift". Many are also calling it "Ascension". Not to be confused with the Christian term and meaning, this metaphysical term refers to a rapid process of awakening from a very dense state of consciousness known as the "Third Dimension" to a much freer and loving state of consciousness called the "Fifth Dimension".

I have written at length about this shift in my two previous books, *Awakening to the Fifth Dimension* and *Ascension: Embracing the Transformation*, and many others have also been writing about it.

The Fifth Dimension

The Fifth Dimension is the level of consciousness many of us have been dreaming about and praying for, perhaps for many lifetimes. In this state of being, we will be able to live in an on-going state of inner peace and joy, unconditional love, and a freedom from fear, shame, judgment and separation. It's a state of being we once existed in many thousands of years ago, before the advent of what's known as the "Fall of Consciousness", a time when we began descending into the lower vibrational field that's the Third Dimension.

This lower dimension is a level of existence in the universe that allowed for a new expression for Consciousness to manifest life in a dense, physical form. But it unfortunately also brought with it many confining limitations: a forgetting of our divine nature, a sense of separation from each other and from the Divine, and experiences of great suffering.

Many of us have been incarnating over and over again into the Earth's Third Dimension for the thousands of years since the Fall of Consciousness. So it is nearly impossible for us to remember the experience of living in the Fifth Dimension. What we remember is the suffering present in this lower dimension and the challenges in remembering who we actually are – powerful, loving, multi-dimensional Beings of Light.

Transitional Times

One of the things the ascension paradigm describes very well is how, in order for this shift into such an evolved level of consciousness to take place, humanity needs first to go through a period of intense transition. All that has been part of the distortions of the third-dimensional consciousness must be purged and left behind.

All the separation, injustice, tyranny, oppression and prejudice that exist in our social and political structures – as well as all the negative mindsets and emotions that have created these structures – must be eliminated. None of it can go with us into the much freer state of consciousness of the Fifth Dimension.

This process of releasing negativity is exactly what we are witnessing and experiencing now -- including all the terrorist attacks and mass shootings that seem to be increasing. It's as if humanity is in a period of "cleanse" or "purification" in which all the toxins that our species has generated over the past thousands of years are now being pushed to the surface in order to be clearly seen, resolved, and then released.

Severe earth changes that have now begun in earnest since the end of 2017 are also part of this purification process: the hurricanes, earthquakes, floods, fires, volcanic eruptions. Severe climate changes are being caused by cosmic rays the sun is streaming toward the earth, all to be expected when traveling through this section of the Milky Way.

Collective Ascension

Some people who are serious about their personal ascension process tend to ignore what's happening out in the world as much as they can. They see it as a distraction from the important inner work they believe they need to be doing. Or it makes them feel depressed or angry, which they believe is not good for keeping their vibration high. All this can be true.

And yet, for full ascension to take place, we need to embrace our awareness of ourselves as part of the human race, as we are all ascending together as a collective of Souls who have chosen to ascend with the Earth at this time. To support this awareness of our collective experience, it is necessary to wake up to what is currently occurring in the world and to what has occurred in the past that originally contributed to the Fall of Consciousness.

This includes becoming aware of the many atrocities that have been perpetrated on us as members of the human race – how we have in many ways given up our sovereign right as a species to determine how we choose to live our lives. As a whole, we have been asleep to the fact that we have not lived in our true reality as the inherently powerful, spiritual Beings we are. And we need to learn how to transform ourselves from victims to sovereign, empowered creators.

To do this, it's essential to be aware of the larger picture of what is happening beyond what mainstream communications and textbooks have traditionally taught us. I'm not just referring to gaining greater political awareness, although this can be a part of the process. It's more a matter of considering humanity as a whole, seeing where we now are as a species that is evolving, and facing some hard truths.

Disclosure

With this goal in mind, it can be helpful to pay attention to the movement of "disclosure" that is currently occurring on multiple sites throughout the internet and at international conferences. The disclosure consists of an enormous amount of essential information that has been purposely kept from the public for decades – and, in some cases, even centuries. It is streaming out from huge numbers of high-level whistle-blowers from the military, governmental agencies, intelligence communities and researchers – and reaches far beyond anything that Snowden or Wikileaks has to date revealed.

Millions of people currently tune into these alternative sources every day. However, many more people world-wide are still only following the news through the mainstream media, which only occasionally reports small and insignificant snippets of the information the whistle-blowers are revealing.

But at some point, it seems, mainstream media sources will have to reveal this information. Disclosure may be gradual, or it could come all at once. But, either way, because of the startling -- and at times very dark -- nature of this information, many people's worldviews and ideas about what is real may be seriously challenged, and their sense of inner security could be greatly impacted.

Misinformation and Disinformation

The information now being revealed is that what we've been taught about humanity's evolution and what has been happening for decades by hidden sources within our governments and social institutions has not only been incomplete, but grossly inaccurate.

To make matters worse, it will be clear that the misinformation has been given deliberately for purposes of manipulation far more devious than most people realize or imagine. This is not news to most thoughtful and informed people; yet the full scope and depth of it may be shocking.

Among other things, it will be revealed that there is a very small group of powerful people who have been running the governments, the military, the media, the global financial structure, and many other public institutions across the planet since ancient times. And that these people have been involved in certain dark activities that are beyond most people's comprehension, such as purposely creating wars, disease and famine – and also participating in actual enslavement through forced labor and sex trafficking. We may also hear that certain high profile politicians and other famous people we have respected and trusted are not who we've believed them to be.

It will also become clear that there is solid evidence that extraterrestrial beings have not only been here with us in our skies for a long, long time, they have also often landed and lived on earth. We will learn about ancient human civilizations that existed many thousands of years prior to what scientists and archeologists currently report; and that in these early civilizations, beings from the outer reaches of the universe lived openly among humans, mated with them, and often dominated them.

Humans in Bondage

Indeed, as you continue to read, you will learn that these dark forces have been controlling, manipulating – and, in essence, enslaving – the human race for eons of time. This may sound like a grossly exaggerated, overly-melodramatic way to describe the human condition. But in reading the information presented in this book, you will undoubtedly realize how accurate the word "slavery" actually is. Indeed, it is heart-breaking to take this truth in. And yet it must be seen, understood and met with full consciousness in order for both liberation and ascension to occur.

As disturbing as it may be to learn the extent of the control and manipulation humanity has been suffering under, you will hopefully also experience how liberating it is, as well – and how many questions are answered about why it is so difficult for humans to come to peace with themselves and one another. It will also hopefully help to create for you an even greater compassion for all of humanity, as well as for yourself. The struggle toward physical, emotional and spiritual liberation has been a very long and difficult one.

If you are new to these ideas, it may all sound like ridiculous science fiction or fantasy stories – or outrageous ideas of "conspiracy theorists". This is understandable. But I invite you to read further and decide later what you decide to think about it.

Misinterpretation of the Disclosure

Of course, not everything that is being disclosed at this point – or that will be in the future – is absolutely true. Aside from the misinformation and disinformation that needs to be sifted through, there is also the inevitable misinterpretation that weaves through the information coming out. It is sometimes difficult to discern what is actually true and what is not. But I believe it is important for us to simply be open to the possibility that what is being disclosed may largely or at least in part be true.

This is an invitation for us to keep an open mind. As we know, many times in the past new information about reality, the earth, or humanity has been revealed – and, inevitably, it is initially dismissed by most people, especially by "experts". But in time, the truth has won out. Although it may take a long time, people tend to eventually come around to recognizing it.

You will see that we are at one of those times in history now, when we will be compelled to make huge shifts in our understanding about how the world actually functions, who humanity is as a species, and what life is all about.

This is all part of the collective evolutionary process that is now unfolding across the planet. It's definitely a wild ride, and sometimes a frightening one. But it can also be seen as a gloriously exciting journey we are all on together at this time. There is no mistake that we chose to incarnate during these years to be part of this cosmic transformation. It's an event many of us have waited for – perhaps for eons of time.

Purpose of This Book

The purpose of this book is to introduce you to the hugely complex web of information now available about the incomplete and gravely distorted version of truth we've all been fed about humanity's history on Earth – and what is still going on behind the scenes. It is to create some psychological preparation for you before or while disclosure is happening, so you can sail through this part of the ascension process with as much ease as possible.

My purpose is to also hopefully give you a sense of hope and empowerment through waking up to these truths – as without this knowledge, it is difficult to face and deal with what it reveals.

At the same time, if possible, I encourage you to maintain some emotional distance while reading the darker aspects of what I will be presenting. See if you can maintain a neutral consciousness about it. Initially, experiencing anger and grief is natural; allow the energy of these feelings to empower you. But try to not dwell on them or get caught in a 3D consciousness of separation, polarization, withdrawal or fear.

If you keep enough distance from it, even the darkest information can be simply seen as fascinating. The whole human drama that's occurred throughout the ages is actually a story that is far more amazing than any science fiction that's ever been written.

I won't be going into great detail with any of the material I present. This has been accomplished by many, many others through books, website posts and videos I will give reference to following each chapter. This book is designed to simply introduce and highlight the important aspects of the wide range of information that is currently being disclosed.

If all this is new to you, you can see this book as a gentle eye-opener. At first, much of it may seem totally far-fetched. But eventually, if you're open and you do your own research on the subjects I present, you'll likely better comprehend the truth within the material, and you'll see that it makes a lot of sense out of the many puzzling events taking place in the world.

In any case, I encourage you to not take my word for anything you read here. After checking the information out for yourself, always tune into your inner guidance to discern the truth. If something doesn't make sense or initially resonate with you, put it on the "shelf". If there is important truth in it for you, it will appear again later.

If you are already aware of much of what I'll be describing, you can use this book as a source that brings much of the information together. It may also assist you in describing the material more effectively to people you know who are currently confused or unaware of it.

I must, however, repeat the caveat that what I've included in this book may or may not be entirely true. I have tried to present only information that has documentation behind it – or to indicate when it does not. Also keep in mind that what I include may no longer be true by the time you read it, as so much is changing so rapidly.

Seeing the Up-Side

But most importantly, I wish to present the up-side of all that is being revealed. Many people writing and talking about this kind of material tend to focus on the negative aspects involved and the horrific stories of how humanity has been manipulated and kept from knowing the truth. In telling these stories, they often speak from a 3D consciousness of separation and anger and an "us vs. them" consciousness.

The stories and facts themselves are important to know and understand. But I'm more interested in focusing on the positive side of what we're learning and in grasping how we are finally being freed at long last to understand who we truly are as the human species. We can discover that we are really much more powerful and amazing Beings than we know and can be in charge of our own lives and the world, as we find our way into the Fifth Dimension.

Powerful Help is Here

Finally, it is significant to note that all the previously hidden information would not be coming out at this time if humanity were not now able to handle it. It is also being revealed because powerful help is finally here to assist us into freedom.

This help has been called the "Light Forces", an alliance of two basic forces. The first consists of a great number of courageous human beings committed to revealing the truth and taking action to address the problems they can assist with on the physical level. And the second part of the alliance is comprised of a multitude of powerful benevolent extraterrestrial beings focused on liberating us on many levels beyond the physical.

Keep this is mind as you come to anything you read in the chapters ahead that shocks or disturbs you. We truly are at the precipice of shifting into a whole new era of our evolution, one in which we will be able to freely express ourselves as the gloriously creative and loving race of Beings that the Archangels, Ascended Masters and highly-evolved ETs have always known us to be.

With this in mind, let us now take a look at what some of the hidden truths have been.

The Global Shift - References

Scientific Evidence of Shift
1. Lipton, Bruce and Bhaerman, Steve. *Spontaneous Evolution: Our Positive Future and a Way to Get There From Here.*
2. Wilcock, David. *Ascension Mysteries.*

Ascension into the Fifth Dimension
1. Frazier, Vidya. *Awakening to the Fifth Dimension.*
2. Frazier, Vidya. *Ascension: Embracing the Transformation.*
3. Frazier, Vidya. Youtube channel:
https://www.youtube.com/results?search_query=vidya+frazier
4. Self, Jim. *What do you Mean the Third Dimension is Going Away?*

Disclosure
1. Wilcock, David. "Endgame – Disclosure and the Final Defeat of the Cabal".
https://www.youtube.com/watch?v=f6YI5U4uSfg
2. Disclosure Websites to check out:
OperationDisclosure.com
PrepareforChange.net
StillnessintheStorm.com
Waking Times.com
WakeupWorld.com
Zerohedge.com
Collective-Evolution.com
Exopolitics.org

Humanity

Controlled and Manipulated

Chapter 2

The Cabal

I wish to make it clear, first off, that none of the information I present in this book has come to me through direct personal experience, so I cannot vouch for its authenticity. I am not an investigative reporter. I have simply pulled together information from numerous sites on the internet and in books written by whistle blowers, researchers, and investigative reporters, as well as some first-hand sources, as you will see in the references I offer at the end of each chapter. All of what I present here, however, does resonate deeply within me and has been confirmed, at least in its essence, by my own inner guidance.

If you decide to do your own research based on the references I list, be aware of all the articles now coming out in retaliation against the huge number of articles revealing the truth the Powers that Be don't want disclosed.

Also be aware of how censorship has now invaded the search engines, youtube channels, facebook and other social media sites. The establishment is panicking and doing what it can to stay in control of information being released on the internet. It demands a lot of discernment on our part to see through this "fake news" war.

Unempowerment

Some of the information in this chapter may be known to you. You may have an understanding that most governments in the world don't actually serve the people they govern. And you likely know that greed and power-seeking in all their various forms have made the world an unjust place, creating great suffering for many.

But perhaps because you feel helpless about doing anything about any of this, you tend to continue passively accepting it and just focus on working hard to make ends meet and create some meaning in your life. Or maybe you've tried to protest certain injustices you see, but you've experienced very little return for these efforts, as little real change ever seems to happen.

Many good-hearted, concerned people focus on the political scene and end up feeling discouraged and impotent. However, what many of them don't realize is that the impact of what they're concentrating on – such as what the president, Congress or other head of state is or isn't doing – occurs at a rather superficial level.

The actions of these political players *do* have an effect on our world. But, when you explore the subject, you discover that these people purportedly in charge of our governments are, in truth, not as much in control of events occurring in the world as we might think. There are people behind the scenes at levels far above these obvious positions of decision-making who actually determine what happens in every area of our lives.

You also find out that the whole political system in most countries – and especially in the United States – is rotten to the core. And it has been, long before people like those in the current administration ever came into power. Just electing different people in another party in the current system is probably not going to make any real difference.

The One Percent

You're probably aware that there's a very small group of people essentially running the world. They've often been called the *One Percent*. Most people aware of this group tend to focus only on the financial control this elite group has. Maybe the control is also seen in the arenas of healthcare and world resources. Or perhaps with internet privacy invasion. Many people wait for Snowden or Wikileaks to do more of what they've already done in exposing the illegal control certain agencies have over the unsuspecting public.

What's not realized is that those things that have been exposed so far are just the tip of the iceberg. And really – has anything actually been done yet to stop what has been disclosed so far?

Although more of us are becoming aware of how humanity has been controlled in certain ways, few are aware of the depth or the full scope of the control this small elite group has had on our governmental structures, the military, our natural resources, the mainstream media, our religious and educational institutions, and the major corporations that essentially own the world.

The Cabal

This elite group has essentially penetrated all aspects of society. They are often referred to as the "Cabal" or the "Illuminati" – and sometimes the "Bilderbergers" or the "Trilateral Commission". They are committed to creating what they've named the "New World Order" within which they expect to assume complete control of humanity.

They comprise a group of people who have not only infiltrated all political arenas; they also show up on boards of every major international corporation (including major media corporations), in high positions in the Vatican, and in all global banking institutions. Some members of this elite group are known publically, but many are not.

Even if you are aware of this group in terms of geopolitical politics and finance, you may not be fully aware that it is extremely organized or that its members generally belong to certain ancient bloodline lineages, such as the Rothschilds, the Rockefellers, and the European Royals.

Secret Societies

One of the ways they can be traced is by researching the secret societies that most of them belong to, such as the Freemasons, the Knights of Malta, and Skull and Bones – and seeing there are many people you'll recognize who have attained the highest degree of power within the societies. This information has been available to the public since the seventeenth century and can easily be found now online.

However, the secrets they hold are not available – not even to members who have not yet attained a high degree of initiation. And yet, whistle-blowers from these societies do tell us that the members' focus is on control, secrecy and power and that creating fear and weakness in humanity is their aim.

It is interesting to note that many US presidents, world leaders and others in highly influential positions in the world belong to the

Masonic Order and that many also happen to be connected to royal bloodlines. In fact it is said that only two US Presidents, Abraham Lincoln and John F. Kennedy, were not either Masons or elite members of other societies; and both of these non-Freemason presidents were assassinated and then replaced with a Freemason president.

More than Just Hoarding the Wealth

As you will see, there is much more to this group than just being powerful and hoarding most of the wealth on the planet. As Francis Conolly reports in his video "JFK to 9/11: Everything is a Rich Man's Trick", the Cabal also chooses presidents and other heads of state. There is clear documentation that they have started and controlled wars, and then have financed both sides.

According to many insiders who have left the Cabal's structure, their game is to turn us against each other through staged events, lies, and manipulation, by pitting race against race, nation against nation, religion against religion, and haves against have-nots. The Cabal has created and controlled terrorist groups, assassinated people who have spoken out against them, and created terrorist incidents. In addition, through advanced technology, the Cabal has controlled some of our weather, causing disastrous storms and droughts.

It's also become clear that they have infiltrated all the major religions throughout the centuries, by introducing distortions into the original teachings and creating new dogma. They are quite clearly engaged in a spiritual war with the rest of humanity; they strive to keep us ignorant that we have souls, that life after death exists, and that our consciousness is powerful.

As we will see in future chapters, some of the most powerful and dangerous secrets they've maintained pertain to secret space programs they've created over which there is absolutely no oversight. These programs are financed by trillions of dollars of taxpayer money. In fact, certain of these people have been in direct contact with extraterrestrials since the 1930s.

In addition, the people running these covert programs have learned to reverse-engineer the advanced technology they have found on crashed ET craft, which they have then systematically used against humanity. This is technology that, if used positively, could conceivably bring all of humanity out of poverty and ill health.

Most informed people are aware that there are dangerous things in the world that threaten our health and lives, such as many pharmaceuticals and vaccinations, HAARP, chemtrails, fluoride, GMOs and other chemical contaminants in the water, food and soil. But they tend to think it's just corporate greed causing this.

Greed does, of course, play a part – but there is evidence that the Cabal has actually aimed to depopulate the earth by purposely creating disease and death through all these various means. They have also engaged in massive efforts of mind control through movies, TV shows and advertising designed to dumb us down and shape the ways we think, feel and understand the world.

Taking all of this together, it's clear that the Cabal's agenda in essence is to rule the world in a way which is described succinctly by the editor of the New World Order website:

> "There is a plan for the world - a New World Order - devised by a British/American/European financial elite of immense wealth and power, with centuries-old historical roots.
>
> "This oligarchy controls the politicians, the courts, the educational institutions, the food, the natural resources, the foreign policies, the economies and the money of most nations. And, they control the major media, which is why we know nothing about them.
>
> "Modern democracy, as we know it, is less than 250 years old. For most of history, except for this brief period, the world has been ruled by powerful elites who wielded absolute power over their societies, controlled the wealth and resources of their known world, and dominated their people by force. The New World Order cabal plans to restore this model of totalitarian rule on a global scale."

Dark Secrets

Something else that may be coming out on mainstream news soon is that mass arrests are currently taking place across the planet of those who have been involved in huge pedophilia rings that have existed for a very long time.

Former head of the Los Angeles FBI, Ted Gunderson, gives a chilling account of cases he worked on for a number of years involving children used in Satanic rites by Cabal members in his video entitled, "Retired Head of the Los Angeles FBI Tells All about Illuminati, Satanism, and Pedophile Rings in the Government".

Another source reporting similar information is the Victurus Libertas website article, "High-Level Politicians Arrested in Huge Pedophile Sting", which outlines how many Cabal members in powerful positions in the world, including many in the entertainment business and religious positions, and some even in the Vatican itself, have been part of these rings.

And there will be more arrests to come. If you haven't yet heard the terms "Pedogate" or "Pizzagate", you probably will soon – along with news about the vast extent of human trafficking and child trafficking that have been rampant within Cabal circles.

But the secrets get even darker than this. To understand these secrets, we're told by multiple insiders that the Cabal – especially those who are known more as the "Illuminati" – tend to have dark religious beliefs centered around Lucifer and hold a profound contempt for the rest of humanity who are not part of this elite group.

Researcher David Wilcock tells us in *Ascension Mysteries* that his insiders reveal that Cabal members are taught from an early age that they are the chosen, special people, superior to all who are not part of their group. Indeed, they believe that everything on the planet belongs to them – including humanity, itself. Preston James, writer for the Veterans Today website, corroborates this and adds a great deal of information on the Cabal's dark activities.

He tells us that family members of the Cabal are trained from childhood in secret societies through savage initiations to erase any conscience they may have been born with. Those reporting tell us that Lucifer is the god they worship. And their rituals done in the god's name are unbelievably cruel and inhuman.

If all this sounds extreme, be aware that there is a great deal of specific detail about these rituals that has been revealed by members who were once part of them and have since left. I don't recommend reading any of this material at length or in detail; it can be very distressing. It's just important to know these beliefs and rituals held as part of the Illuminati's religion are real and will hopefully soon be revealed for what they are and terminated.

Powerful Negative ETs in Charge

It may seem too fantastical to believe, but you will also see in later chapters that the Cabal actually originated in ancient times through a process of inter-breeding with a number of powerful ETs who had arrived on earth. These particular ETs had an agenda to basically enslave humanity and they have used their human offspring – the Cabal – to do this.

All of this sounds so much like science fiction and "conspiracy theory", that it may be hard to keep a straight face in even considering it. And yet, it all comes from a multitude of whistle-blowers from inside the Cabal and the secret space programs who believe strongly that this information needs to be disclosed to the public at this time.

And if these revelations aren't convincing, be aware that your reaction of disbelief is exactly how the Cabal wants you to react. They've manipulated the way this kind of information has come out in the form of movies, TV shows and comic books, so that we will dismiss it as crazy and/or fictitious and thus stay powerless in our ignorance.

I suggest you try to stay open and see if it might ring true in the end. You may find that your gut tells you something different from what your rational mind believes. Our minds have all been conditioned by lies and misinformation.

In doing this, you can be part of a tremendous collective awakening that is occurring on the planet. You can take in the bad news about all the control and oppression that we have been living under for a very long time. And you can also remember the good news about the powerful alliances at work that are at long last destroying the power of the Cabal – and in many cases, even the Cabal members themselves, if they don't cooperate in letting go of their power. This process has been happening for a number of years now, and at this point much is currently turning around.

The Power of Positive Consciousness

I invite you to consider that the information I give here is not a rant against the "bad guys" or an exhortation to rise up against them. As I've indicated, there are those already committed to doing that. What we as "ordinary" people can focus on is the power of our consciousness to combat our powerlessness and to grasp the potential power of humanity as a whole.

First of all, let's face it: we certainly have the numbers. There are a great many more of us than those in the Cabal. And, secondly, we also have the ability to create and build a consciousness of Light that, when strong enough, can assist in destroying the entire corrupt system and help us to begin to take power over our lives.

So we can help turn things around primarily through informed awareness of what's really going on beneath the surface. It's been said, "We can't dismantle the cage until we see it." Then we can hold an intention to step free of passive acceptance of our powerlessness and take action.

If so inclined, we can act through political involvement or by directly assisting people on the physical level. But we can also act by consciously staying positive in our thoughts and actions, no matter what is going on. We can stay loving and kind and treat others respectfully, no matter who they are. Large groups of people doing this can have an enormous effect on what occurs in the world.

Indeed, we are told by the "Light Forces" that our positive consciousness across the planet is extremely important to them. They use this consciousness as a "battery" to assist them in effectively clearing the Cabal's control from the planet.

It's important to realize that to fully wake up out of third-dimensional consciousness, we need to be able to imagine clearly what it would be like to live in a world without a small elite class of powerful people running it and subjugating the rest of the population to their control. This situation does not exist in the Fifth Dimension or above.

We've lived with this condition of corruption and oppression for so long, it can feel like it could never change. But it can. And we can help bring it about by vividly imagining it. Indeed, we can learn to *remember* a world without corruption or domination, as most of us have previously lived in a Fifth Dimension civilization long, long ago.

It's a matter of stepping outside of the matrix of the third-dimensional reality and truly feeling what a new fifth-dimensional world might be like. What would it feel like for you to wake up in the morning to a world that is not run by a corrupt elite? What would be different? How would this affect your life?

If enough of us can imagine this clearly and begin to live our lives from within this consciousness, we can help bring this new reality forward as quickly as possible.

* * *

The next few chapters will take a closer look at the specific ways in which the Cabal has maintained control over the major institutions in the world and, to some extent, over how we think and experience our lives. These chapters can serve to bring it all together to help you realize the full scope of the control and manipulation that the human race has been subjected to.

The Cabal - References

Internet Censorship

1. Amnesty International website. "Freedom of Expression and the Internet". https://www.amnestyusa.org/themes/business-human-rights/internet-censorship/
2. Anguin, Julia, et al. "Facebook's Secret Censorship Rules Protect White Men from Hate Speech But Not Black Children". https://www.propublica.org/article/facebook-hate-speech-censorship-internal-documents-algorithms
3. Damon, Andre. "Google's chief search engine legitimizes new censorship algorithm". https://www.wsws.org/en/articles/2017/07/31/goog-j31.html

Overview of the Cabal / Illuminati

1. Anderson, Jake. "The New World Order should more accurately be called the Deep State". http://theantimedia.org/forget-the-new-world-order/
2. Boylan, Richard. "The Cabal: A Geoplutocratic Elite Bent on Global Domination". https://www.bibliotecapleyades.net/sociopolitica/sociopol_cabalelite.htm
3. Brown, Kaylee. "An In-Depth Look at the Deep State & Shadow Government". http://www.collective-evolution.com/2017/06/21/an-in-depth-look-at-the-deep-state-shadow-government/
4. Real World Order website. "Real World Order: Who Rules the World?" http://www.realworldorder.net/
5. Gates, Robert, Sr. *The Conspiracy That Will Not Die: How the Rothschild Cabal Is Driving America Into One World Government.* https://www.amazon.com/Conspiracy-That-Will-Not-Die/dp/1934956406
6. Humans are Free website: "Mayer Amschel Rothschild: the Architect of the Illuminati". http://humansarefree.com/2017/08/mayer-amschel-rothschild-architect-of.html?utm_source=feedburner&utm_medium=email&utm_campaign=Feed%3A+humansarefree%2FaQPD+%28Humans+Are+Free%29
7. James, Preston. Overview of the Deep-State, Secret Space Program, Military-Industrial Complex -- The Coming Shift to Cosmic Fascism (Part I, II & III) http://www.stillnessinthestorm.com/2017/06/overview-of-the-deep-state-secret-space-program-military-industrial-complex-the-coming-shift-to-cosmic-fascism-parti.html?utm_source=feedburner&utm_medium=email&utm_campaign=Feed%3A+StillnessInTheStormBlog+%28Stillness+in+the+Storm+Blog%29
8. Shipp, Kevin. "CIA Agent Whistleblower Risks All To Expose The Shadow Government". https://www.youtube.com/watch?v=XHbrOg092GA

9. Wilcock, David. *Ascension Mysteries,* pg.354.
https://www.amazon.com/Ascension-Mysteries-Revealing-Cosmic-Between-ebook/dp/B0191ZL2EC

Secret Space Programs
1. Greer, Steven. "When Disclosure Serves Secrecy".
http://siriusdisclosure.com/cseti-papers/when-disclosure-serves-secrecy/
2. Greer, Steven. http://www.disclosureproject.org/
3. Greer, Steven. *Extraterrestrial Contact: The Evidence and Implications.*
4. Wilcock, David. Ascension "Mysteries: Cosmic Battle between Good and Evil". https://www.youtube.com/watch?v=7-ZWzwNMsxQ
5. Wilcock, David. *Ascension Mysteries: Revealing the Cosmic Battle between Good and Evil.* https://www.amazon.com/Ascension-Mysteries-Revealing-Cosmic-Between-ebook/dp/B0191ZL2EC

Lies, Manipulation
1. Conolly, Francis Richard. "JFK to 9/11. Everything is a Rich Man's Trick". https://www.youtube.com/watch?v=U1Qt6a-vaNM&t=883s
2. Sarich, Christina. "10 Ways the Global Cabal is Controlling You: Part One". http://www.collective-evolution.com/2015/07/05/10-ways-the-global-cabal-is-controlling-you-part-one/

Cabal Manipulating Health
1. Brown, Kalee. "10 Colossal False Health Claims Made By Big Pharma & Mainstream Media".
http://www.collective-evolution.com/2017/06/09/10-colossal-false-health-claims-made-by-big-pharma-mainstream
media/?utm_source=feedburner&utm_medium=email&utm_campaign=Fe
ed%3A+Collective-evolution+%28Collective+Evolution%29
2. Perdomo, Daniella. "100,000 Americans Die Each Year from Prescription Drugs, While Pharma Companies Get Rich"
http://www.alternet.org/story/147318/100%2C000_americans_die_eac
h_year_from_prescription_drugs%2C_while_pharma_companies_get_rich

Dark Secrets
1. BP. "Dutch Elite Banker Blows the Whistle on the Illuminati Banking System" http://www.stillnessinthestorm.com/2017/04/dutch-elite-banker-blows-the-whistle-on-the-illuminati-banking-system-video-transcript.html
2. Gunderson, Ted. "Retired Head of the Los Angeles FBI All about Illuminati, Satanism, and Pedophile Rings in the Government".
http://www.anongroup.org/retired-fbi-govt/
3. James, Preston. "Satanic Pedophile Cabal's Iron Grip of Evil".
http://www.veteranstoday.com/2016/12/04/satanic-pedophile-cabals-iron-grip-of-evil/

Pizzagate/Pedogate

1. Jones, Alex. "Pedogate Arrests Begin to Pile Up".
https://www.youtube.com/watch?v=pW6qNPeFkK0
2. Washington, Christian. "The Shocking Truth Why Pope Benedict
Resigned." https://www.youtube.com/watch?v=ztisTKy2KTE
3. Wilcock, David. "Endgame and Final Defeat of the Cabal".
http://divinecosmos.com/start-here/davids-blog/1208-endgame-pt-1

Negative ET Influence

1. Calise, Greg. "The Enslavement of Souls and the Archon Gate Keepers".
http://humansarefree.com/2017/07/the-enslavement-of-souls-and-
archon.html
2. Cobra. "Earth in Quarantine". http://prepareforchange.net/earth-
quarantine-last-26000-years/
3. Wilcock, David. *Ascension Mysteries*, pg. 354.
https://www.amazon.com/Ascension-Mysteries-Revealing-Cosmic-
Between-ebook/dp/B0191ZL2EC

Chapter 3

Financial Control

It's common knowledge that the "One Percent" holds most of the world's money and maintains control over the financial structures that run the global economy.

Although this dynamic affects the entire world population, I will be presenting information here that mostly pertains to the United States, as this country has had the strongest global economic control over the last century. Just recently, this situation has begun to change with moves that China and Russia have made with the BRICS Alliance (Brazil, Russia, India, China and So. Africa) behind them. But change on this geopolitical level is usually slow.

2008 Bail-Outs

We can all remember the huge bail-out of the large US banks that occurred back in 2008 when those banks themselves caused a serious recession, creating huge repercussions and losses for the American population at the time.

A number of videos and films have told this story of "too big to fail" corporations, all of which were owned and controlled by the Cabal. Although many thousands of Americans were drastically affected by the recession, losing their homes and life savings, only the banks and the Cabal who owned them were rescued by the bail-outs.

At the time of the bail-outs, the mainstream media reported that the costs to taxpayers added up to about $1.2 trillion. There were those who indicated that bailing banks out "is what a central bank (the Federal Reserve in the US) is supposed to do." This seemed like an outrageous amount of money to be given to banks. But it was revealed later that the actual sum was a great deal higher than had been reported.

Thanks to the efforts of former Congressman Ron Paul, former Congressman Alan Grayson, and Congressman Bernie Sanders, the Federal Reserve was finally audited. It is now known that the Federal Reserve secretly lent out 26 trillion dollars' worth of US money from 2007 to 2010.

The four largest recipients were Citigroup, Morgan Stanley, Merrill Lynch and Bank of America, each of whom received more than a trillion dollars each. Additional money was lent to a number of foreign banks, each receiving between a quarter trillion to a trillion dollars, at zero percent interest. As of 2012, none of this money had been returned.

Financial Tyranny

In his article "Financial Tyranny", researcher David Wilcock showed that if the $26 trillion that was given to the banks would have been distributed instead to every man, woman and child living in America at the time, each of them would have received $100,000.

In addition to the revelation of the true amount of the bail-out, it was revealed that the Federal Reserve owns the financial agencies they are supposed to be regulating. The people "regulating" the banks are the exact same people who are being "regulated".

Add to all this the fact that the Federal Reserve notes most people think are printed and controlled by the US Treasury aren't even backed by gold. The Federal Reserve simply keeps printing as much money as they wish out of thin air. And then add the fact that the US government is in huge debt to the Federal Reserve – a private corporation owned by the Cabal that has utterly no oversight.

You will remember the powerful spontaneous protest to the bail-outs that began through a grassroots movement calling itself "Occupy Wall Street" and which spawned a number of other similar protest movements; and yet, as usual, nothing much tangible came of these protests in the end. Even after the gigantic efforts that congressmen and others have made to expose the Cabal through the audits they brought about, nothing has been done about the situation. Nor have there been any significant arrests for fraud or other wrong-doing.

Something that has become more and more obvious ever since that recession is that the middle class in the US has actually been disappearing. More and more people, including those who are well-educated and young, have been falling below the poverty line – either because they are unable to find employment or they're working at multiple jobs for minimum wage. Both inflation and overwhelming debt have pulled these people under, and more and more have been forced to file bankruptcy than ever before.

It is reported that millions in the US are now out of work and have lost their homes. However, there are other sources that say these figures are inaccurate – that up to ten percent of the potential workforce is now either unemployed or has given up all search for employment. Many jobs are simply not available anymore due to out-sourcing and robotics.

A number of different sources describe the current global economy as gravely unstable and are predicting, in particular, a huge crash of the US dollar in the near future, despite current thriving stock market numbers. Only time will tell if this prediction comes to pass, but it's probably safe to be alert to this possibility.

The Federal Reserve

To fully grasp the situation, it's important to understand how the US pulled off the bail-outs. Where did the money come from to do this?

You may believe that US currency is printed by the US Treasury. This is not accurate. Since 1913, currency of the US has been owned and managed by a private corporation of international Cabal bankers known as the Federal Reserve System. This corporation is not a part of the United States government. It prints "Federal Reserve Notes" which it lends to the US Treasury.

The Feds pay a few cents for each bill they print, whatever its denomination, and then charges the government at the bills' face value, plus interest. In essence, the American taxpayers pay interest to the Federal Reserve banking families for the rights to use their money.

Additionally, the Federal Reserve bankers can print as much money as they wish, and give it to whomever they want, without any oversight or input from the US government. Former Federal Reserve Chairman, Alan Greenspan, described the situation clearly: "The Federal Reserve is an independent agency. And that means basically that there is no other agency of government which can overrule actions that we take."

There is an excellent film by Foster and Kimberly Gamble called "Thrive" in which the dynamics of the Federal Reserve are very clearly described. Other informed articles on the subject can also be found online.

Financial Slavery

So it's relatively easy to grasp the situation at the apparent level of facts and statistics. But the whole financial reality can also be seen from a more insidious perspective, if you step back to look at the system from a greater distance and see what financial control actually creates in our everyday lives. This requires shifting out of all programmed beliefs about money, work, and what you believe is necessary for people to live.

In his book, *Modern Slavery,* Edmund Morgan offers a clear perspective of the financial control we're all under: "In our current society, we have more choice than ever – but do we have true freedom? Many elements of our society seem more like a form of modern slavery". He adds that "slavery" might be a strong word to use, but asserts that certain parallels can actually be drawn between physical slavery and the financial system we live with. And we must see these parallels if we are to attain true freedom.

First, it's important to step out of the belief we've all grown up with that work of some kind is necessary for survival (unless you happen to be one of the privileged few to be born to great wealth or are granted it later in life). This is a belief based on our current and historical experience living in the reality known as the Third Dimension, which is a level of reality in which limitation and oppression are dominant. There are other levels of reality in which this notion of having to work to survive simply does not exist.

This is especially important to realize if you're someone who is like many people who have to work long hours at jobs that are exhausting and soul-destroying, often for a low wage that isn't even sustainable. Or if you're someone who's had to take on additional jobs simply to make ends meet – while your employers are raking in huge profits from the work you're doing.

This is essentially slavery. And it's hard to escape this situation when there are so many bills to pay. Most expenses are not optional. Money is needed for heat, light, water, medical care, gas and food – on top of rent or mortgage – plus all the other necessities. Many stores people shop at happen to be owned by the same corporations they work for, so they end up paying money back to the same people who paid them for working. It's important to see the insanity of all this. And to realize it need not be this way.

GESARA

Much has been written and spoken about an act called GESARA – an acronym for "Global Economic Security & Reformation Act". The act is designed, among other things, to reset the planet and humanity on a sustainable governance foundation and benefit everyone on the planet through a global currency reset (the GCR). It would put the entire global economy back on the gold standard. If implemented, it would affect all 209 sovereign nations in the world.

It is said that this act has been written and refined over a period of many years. Economists have also referred to NESARA, which is the US version of the act. Among other things, NESARA would provide for the dismantling of the Federal Reserve, along with its collection arm, the IRS. Some sources say that NESARA was almost implemented at certain times in past years in the United States, but that it was ultimately blocked by the Cabal at those times.

Others have indicated that GESARA was buried within the 2015 Paris Agreement on Climate Change that all 209 sovereign nations signed. This may or may not be true, as there is no real evidence that there was anything explicit in this Agreement that spelled any of this out.

Indeed, it's hard to know if these acts have actually gotten any further than the proposal stages, as I have not encountered many documented reports that can be validated about them. However, there are many references to them by a number of sources, some of them insiders in governmental agencies. There are evidently those who are intent on eventually implementing acts like these when the time is right.

Financial Karma Being Balanced

It's important to note that there have been some signs that certain elite banking corporations have been investigated and charged in recent years with financial crimes. Author of *The*

Transfiguration of our World, Gordon Asher Davidson, points out that in 2015, JP Morgan was made to pay a $13 billion settlement for knowingly selling bad loans packaged as securities to unwitting investors. And currency traders at Citibank, Barclays, JP Morgan and US were being investigated by international officials for rigging the $5.3 trillion a day foreign exchange market with major fines levied against them.

Davidson further describes how there is one nation in the world, Costa Rica, that has resisted the Cabal's financial control for a number of years. Costa Rican banks have been publicly owned for the last 66 years, in spite of enormous pressure by the IMF to privatize them.

Breaking Free of Financial Control

But until there are more signs of positive change in the global financial structure, it seems it is up to us to help bring about reform in whatever way we can in our lives. For example, there are towns and communities in which people use alternative currency for many products and services. Although the IRS has attempted to intervene in different ways with these systems, it has not generally been successful.

Buying Bitcoin is another way people are attempting to get around the current financial system. This alternative currency allows all transactions to be made with no middle men, banks, or transaction fees and no need to give your real name.

But again, there is another resource that many of us can use to bring the current financial system down and that is through the power of our consciousness. We can actively and vividly imagine a world in which everyone is free to live their lives without financial stress. We can hold the vision of what an Earth existing in the Fifth Dimension would be like, where there is abundance of everything, and financial survival simply is not an issue. Indeed, we can embrace the likelihood that the whole notion of money itself or having to work to survive simply does not exist on any level of consciousness higher than the Fourth Dimension.

What would it be like for you to not "have" to work to survive? What would you do? If you enjoy working, your work could be exactly what you'd love to do, what gives you joy. It could be freely creative and designed to fully support the values you hold. You would be free to express and enjoy your passions, whatever they are.

This is the world we are actually moving toward, as the ascension of the Earth and humanity continues to take hold. But because of our innate power to create, our consistently imagining it and learning how to hold it in our awareness at all times will bring it about all the faster.

Financial Control – References

Cabal and Financial Control
1. Bernard, Ronald. "All Misery on Earth is a Business Model".
https://www.youtube.com/watch?v=5pXKrWj9ZuE
2. BP. "Dutch Elite Banker Blows the whistle on the Illuminati Banking
System". http://www.stillnessinthestorm.com/2017/04/dutch-elite-
banker-blows-the-whistle-on-the-illuminati-banking-system-video-
transcript.html
3. James, Preston. "The Coming Shift to Cosmic Fascism-Part III"
http://www.veteranstoday.com/2017/05/24/the-coming-shift-to-
cosmic-fascism-part-iii/
4. Keefe, Patrick Radden. "Limited Liability: Why don't corporate
wrongdoers get charged?". "The New Yorker", July 31, 2017.
5. Klein, Naomi. *The Shock Doctrine: The Rise of Disaster Capitalism.*
https://www.amazon.com/Shock-Doctrine-Rise-Disaster-
Capitalism/dp/0312427999
6. Editor, Learning-Mind.com website. "Modern Slavery: 5 Tools Today's
Society uses to take away our Freedom".
https://www.learning-mind.com/modern-slavery-
society/?utm_source=feedburner&utm_medium=email&utm_campaign=F
eed%3A+LearningMind+%28Learning+Mind+email%29
7. Morgan, Edmund: *American Slavery, American Freedom.*
https://www.amazon.com/American-Slavery-Freedom-Edmund-
Morgan/dp/039332494X
8. Wilcock, David. "Financial Tyranny".
http://divinecosmos.com/start-here/davids-blog/1023-financial-tyranny

2008 Bail-Outs – Too Big to Fail
1. Hanson, Curtis, Director. "Too Big to Fail" film.
http://www.imdb.com/title/tt1742683/
2. Sorkin, Andrew Ross. Too Big to Fail: The Inside Story of How Wall
Street and Washington Fought to Save the Financial System--and
Themselves.

Federal Reserve
1. Lehrer, Jim. "Greenspan Examines Federal Reserve, Mortgage Crunch".
**http://www.pbs.org/newshour/bb/business-july-dec07-
greenspan_09-18/**
2. Maran, Daniel. "What The Federal Reserve Would Look Like If
Progressives Had Their Way".
http://www.huffingtonpost.com/entry/progressive-federal-reserve-
reform-proposal_us_570c0a51e4b014223249dcd8

GESARA
"What is GESARA"? http://www.theeventchronicle.com/study/what-is-
gesara/

Positive Signs of Financial Karma Being Balanced
Davidson, Gordon Asher. *The Transfiguration of our World.*
https://www.amazon.com/Transfiguration-Our-World-Alliance-Transforming/dp/0983569134/ref=sr_1_1?s=books&ie=UTF8&qid=1507706651&sr=1-1&keywords=Gordon+Asher+Davidson

Disappearing Middle Class
White, Martha C. So Long, Middle Class: Middle Income Jobs are Disappearing the Fastest".
http://www.nbcnews.com/business/economy/so-long-middle-class-middle-income-jobs-are-disappearing-fastest-n623886

Guaranteed Basic Income
Raphael, T. J. "Finland's guaranteed basic income is working to tackle poverty" May 15, 2017. https://www.pri.org/stories/2017-05-06/finlands-guaranteed-basic-income-working-tackle-poverty

Chapter 4

Political Control

We all pretty much know that the US government lies to us. This is not new; you probably kind of take it for granted. Perhaps you occasionally get angry about it. But you likely feel powerless to do anything about it so you just tend to either complain about it or simply ignore it.

But you may not be aware of the actual extent of the corruption that takes place within the government. You may not realize just how much the Cabal has run the government from the very beginning, even when the country was first established. And how it has only gotten more powerful as time has gone on.

What I present here is not designed to create more anger or polarization, or a further sense of powerlessness. It's intended to hopefully bring you greater awareness so that you can fully understand the scope of what is now beginning to turn around as the world shifts toward the Fifth Dimension – and to see how you can perhaps contribute to this turn-around.

The US is a Corporation

So first let's start with the myth most Americans believe: that the US is a republic. It actually isn't – it's a corporation. When the US government refers to the United States, ninety-nine percent of the time it is referring to the corporation known as the "United States, Inc.".

Furthermore, the US government is basically a corporate instrument of a group of Cabal-owned international banks. This corporation did not appear overnight. It was built slowly, with stealth, and took over 150 years to create.

Real History of the US Government

To understand what the US federal government has actually become, it's necessary to review the history that does not appear in most history books. What you will find through research, for example, is that the original Constitution of 1781 was hijacked just after the Civil War and that a new one was put in its place.

On Feb 21, 1871, the "Act of 1871" was passed in Congress. This act formed the corporation known as "The United States, Inc.". Congress, allegedly under no constitutional authority to do so, essentially threw out the original Constitution.

To give them their due, Congress did this because of the dire financial straits the US government was in, brought about by the Civil War. But how they did it remains a sad fact to this day. The way they obtained the money to keep the country afloat was to borrow it from a group of international bankers of the time, which mainly consisted of European Cabal members – but who were closely connected to the Cabal members already in place in the US government.

Through this act, in return for their money, these bankers got their foot in the door to eventually take over both the financial and political affairs of the US. Part of how they did this was by transforming the US government into a corporation, which was then subject to all the laws for corporations, rather than to those for sovereign nations.

Then, shortly after the Civil War, the new corporation of The USA, Inc. passed a law granting corporations the rights of "persons". And later, in 1913, it turned the control of US credit and currency over to the same international bankers it had borrowed money from, by passing the Federal Reserve Act.

This then gave the bankers the ability to turn the US Treasury Department (including all its assets) over to the Federal Reserve – which, as we've seen, was a private corporation run by the Cabal. These actions, in essence, allowed the Cabal to fully step in and control the most important issues the government deals with.

Something else most people don't know is that the federal government went bankrupt in 1933. So, after pillaging and bankrupting the country, the Federal Reserve cartel turned over the entire country – including the people – as collateral on its corporate debt and bound the individual states to its bankruptcy obligations.

Among other things, the government did this through issuing birth certificates and Social Security numbers and inventing a number of licenses that were required by the government (such as hunting, marriage, and dog licenses, etc.). These regulations essentially made Americans into registered "collateral" for the payment of the debt owed to the banking cartel.

This may sound like a radical exaggeration of the facts, but some sources have actually referred to this act as one that essentially made the American people "chattel" of the US Corporation. Among other things, it explains the need for income tax and where much of our tax money goes – into the pockets of those who "own" us.

True Story behind Wars

Growing up as we have in this 3D world of strife and conflict, we have become almost immune to the tragedies and feelings of grief we naturally experience about the horror that wars create. It seems like a simple fact of life: war is inevitable – it's just human nature and it's been happening since time began.

This may appear to be so. But what if you discovered that war actually is not inevitable? That most people in the world really do not want it? And that it's the Cabal that has inevitably, behind the scenes, brought it about in the last few centuries?

According to many testimonies, some from whistle-blowers who grew up in Cabal bloodline families, one of the basic tactics they use to increase their wealth is by creating war between countries or factions in opposition. Not only is war "good for business", it also helps to keep people in fear and therefore weak and submissive. In addition, it serves to reduce the world population. All good for tightening the Cabal's control over humanity.

They do this very systematically and cleverly, understanding people's weaknesses. First, they manage to intentionally cause strife between nations, cultures, religions, races or sexes. Then they find angry and unempowered men they can train and pay to be leaders and followers of operations that will ignite the conflicts.

And then, once the war begins, unbelievably, they also finance both sides of the war they've created. This happened, in particular, when certain of the American Cabal wealthy families helped to not only create the conflicts leading to WWII, but also to finance the war machinery – planes, tanks, weapons – for the Nazis as well as for the Allies once it began.

Political Rigging

So understanding all this, it's not a big leap to assume that political rigging has also been going on for quite a while by the Cabal groups. You may be aware of the warning that Eisenhower gave about the "military-industrial complex" in his final speech as president. But the fact is we've been warned by a number of past presidents, vice presidents, congressmen, senators and other high profile political leaders over the last 214 years about the Cabal's control.

Many have spoken about the "Invisible Government" that had taken hold of the US government – and how this government owes no allegiance to the people of the US and acknowledges no responsibility to them. And it's been clear in certain cases that the political leaders, themselves, have been fearful of this invisible government. Indeed, together, these historical figures paint a pretty dire picture of our democracy, asserting that the invisible government is the true ruling power in our country.

A well-researched article by Ross Pittman, "Dire Warnings from Past U.S. Presidents and Other High-Profile Leaders about an Invisible Government", presents quotes from many political leaders throughout US history, from George Washington to John Kennedy. Here are just a few statements of the political leaders quoted in the article:

Thomas Jefferson in a letter to a colleague: "I sincerely believe, with you, that banking establishments are more dangerous than standing armies."

Theodore Roosevelt: "Behind the ostensible government sits enthroned an invisible government owing no allegiance and acknowledging no responsibility to the people."

Woodrow Wilson: "We have come to be one of the worst ruled, one of the completely controlled and dominated, governments in the civilized world – no longer a government by free opinion, no longer a government by conviction and the vote of the majority, but a government by the opinion and the duress of small groups of dominant men."

FDR: "...a financial element in the large centers has owned the government ever since the days of Andrew Jackson."

JFK: In a quote from his 1961 "Secret Society Speech":

> " ... For we are opposed around the world by a monolithic and ruthless conspiracy that relies primarily on covert means for expanding its sphere of influence – on infiltration instead of invasion, on subversion instead of elections, on intimidation instead of free choice, on guerrillas by night instead of armies by day."

JFK was the last president to speak publicly of the dangerous group of men running the world, and it is said by some that he was probably assassinated for doing so.

As always, despite these warnings by highly-respected leaders, no one has been able to do anything about the fact that the US has been covertly controlled by the invisible government, even from the very beginning.

The Office of the President Has Little Power

Indeed, it's clear to many sources that anyone in a political office, including that of the US president, has little power over making important decisions about the country – that, if they are not part of the Cabal, themselves (and even then), they are essentially under the control of this very small and powerful elite group.

Insiders who have left this group claim that to the Cabal, presidents are just public figureheads which they've basically chosen, themselves, since they are in control of both political parties. Presidents are often kept deliberately ignorant and given very little access to real secrets. In addition, the Cabal is evidently masterful at pinning blame on people in elected offices, thereby diverting it from themselves.

In fact, if a president wishes to make his own decisions about certain issues, he is routinely threatened with dire consequences if he refuses to do what he is told by this covert group.

A heart-rending story was told about President Obama by one of Wilcock's White House insiders. It was about a private meeting Obama was invited to by several former presidents, including both Bushes, which took place right before Obama's inauguration, and to which no press were invited.

It's reported that during the meeting, Obama was verbally abused and also seriously threatened that if he didn't follow the orders given from certain powerful international bankers, he and his family would be in grave danger. Someone happened to see him as he emerged from that meeting, totally shaken. Apparently believing himself to be alone, he evidently stumbled over to a chair and collapsed into it, putting his head in his hands, weeping.

Corruption at the Primary Level

Much has been written and spoken about the corruption that occurred during the Democratic Primaries in 2016 – and how Hillary "stole" the nomination from Bernie Sanders. There was much disclosure in the alternative media at the time about what took place both during and afterward through the collection of DNC emails leaked to Wikileaks in July 2016, and tremendous protest eventually arose in response to it.

The then FBI Director Comey confused the whole issue by releasing information the FBI had about Hillary and then essentially withdrawing it; but this confusing activity only proved the likelihood that something fishy about Hillary and the DNC was going on.

And yet, it tended to not get the attention it deserved, as the nation was more focused at that point on the chaos the Republican Party's mind-boggling choices of candidates was creating. And, because for years the Democratic Party had been the party liberals had traditionally chosen due to the principles it espoused, they couldn't imagine that this party might be infiltrated and controlled by the very corrupt and self-serving kinds of people they had always despised.

It has since become clear, however, that the DNC had indeed been infiltrated. Although at one point they had consistently denied any corruption of the democratic process during the primaries, former DNC Chair Debbie Wasserman-Schultz finally revealed that the party establishment did ensure that Hillary Clinton would win the presidential nomination against Sen. Bernie Sanders by rigging the primaries.

Of course, there is rampant corruption within the Republican Party, as well. And even more is being revealed as time goes on – deceits, lies and manipulations, some possibly illegal, that were exposed during the election and continue to today. It's clear that the whole two-party system is fraught with corruption.

Help from within the System

As in certain other arenas currently still controlled by the "Deep State", as the invisible government is sometimes called, there are now powerful movements gaining momentum within the political system, itself, aimed at rectifying the current existing structure. One team that has come together with this goal is an unlikely match of a former Civil Rights Congresswoman and a former CIA spy. Dr. Cynthia McKinney and Robert David Steele have outlined a simple, inexpensive game plan for restoring integrity to the US election process based on a "manifesto" composed by Steele, called *Beyond Trump & Sanders*.

Their aim is to bring the Alt-Right and the Alt-Left together at the Congressional district level with people of color, Greens, Libertarians, other interested parties and "the 50% who are Independent" to talk about the manifesto and their proposed Election Reform Act of 2017. They plan to team up with a broad range of politicians, world leaders and activists to create a movement that has nothing to do with the "Two-Party scam" that currently runs the US political system.

Another powerful movement gaining momentum is led by passionate Bernie Sanders supporters who still believe something can be done within the system, by fervently supporting a new generation of progressive leaders. Calling themselves "Our Revolution", they are striving to empower millions to fight for progressive change and elevate political consciousness.

Some within the movement are emphasizing the need to bring in and train more women as local and national candidates. Others spend time recruiting Millennials, who, according to recent polls, appear to be bringing in a higher consciousness about the way the world should be run.

Iceland Leads the Way

Whether anyone is able to bring true integrity into the workings of the US government from within the current system remains to be seen. If not, a non-violent revolution may need to happen from outside the system.

We have a beautiful example of how this happened in another country. In 2009, a large group of extremely disgruntled Icelanders gathered and actually walked into their version of a Congress and essentially fired everyone there. They then managed to send several bankers to jail who had forced Iceland into bankruptcy – and then further told the international bankers Iceland was in debt to that their country would not be paying back a debt that they, the people, had never sanctioned. After spending a few months writing up a plan for a new constitutional system, they then held elections under this new system.

Of course, Iceland is a small, homogeneous country. This particular method of quiet revolution would be hard to pull off in a country as large and divisive as the US. But perhaps it can be done in a different way. With the right consciousness of fairness, integrity and justice – coupled with empowerment – there may be a way. Especially if we start at the local, grassroots level.

Avoiding Polarization

It is difficult to get involved in the political process and not fall into polarization, with a righteous attitude about what we feel is right and wrong. It has been common to take that kind of stance in politics.

But if we are to truly help usher in a new era of peace, compassion and justice, we need to remain above the fray as much as possible. We need to consistently be led by the wisdom of our Hearts in all we say and do regarding how our country is currently run – or we are simply creating more of the same divisive consciousness we wish to eradicate.

Political Control – References

US as a Corporation
1. Anticorruption Society. "Information was compiled as an educational tool." http://anticorruptionsociety.com/is-our-government-just-another-corporation/
2. Chang, Pau, "Proof that the United States is a Criminal Corporation". https://wakeup-world.com/2015/12/02/proof-that-the-usa-is-controlled-by-foreign-corporations/
3. Editor, *State of the Nation website*. "$14.3 Quadrillion Lien Taken Against All U.S. Land, Real Estate and People on July 28, 2011". http://stateofthenation2012.com/?p=79170
4. Giuliani, Lisa. "The United States isn't a Country—It's a Corporation!" http://www.serendipity.li/jsmill/us_corporation.htm
5. Shrout, Winston. "The Goldfish Report No. 115: Country Roads with Winston Shrout". https://youtu.be/U39LKEpho9o

Cabal in the US and Wars
1. Conolly, Francis R. "JFK to 9/11: Everything is a Rich Man's Trick". https://www.youtube.com/watch?v=U1Qt6a-vaNM
2. Physicians for Social Responsibility. "Casualty Figures after 10 Years of the War on Terror" file:///C:/Users/Owner/Downloads/body-count.pdf
3. Stone, Oliver and Kuznick, Peter. *The Untold History of the US*. https://www.amazon.com/Untold-History-United-States/dp/1491512563

Cabal Chooses Presidents
Pittman, Ross. "Former Presidents Warn About the "Invisible Government" Running the United States" http://www.wakingtimes.com/2013/09/13/former-presidents-warn-about-the-invisible-government-running-united-states/

Warnings by Presidents
1. Pittman, Ross. "Dire Warnings from Past U.S. Presidents and Other High-Profile Leaders about an 'Invisible Government' that Runs the U.S. with No Allegiance to the People". http://consciouslifenews.com/verified-warnings-presidents-about-invisible-government-running-allegiance-people/1136001/
2. Satayana, George. "Former Presidents Warn About the "Invisible Government" Running the United States". http://www.wakingtimes.com/2013/09/13/former-presidents-warn-about-the-invisible-government-running-united-states/

Presidents Have Little Power
1. Greer, Steven. *Unacknowledged: An Expose of the World's Greatest Secret*. https://www.amazon.com/Unacknowledged-Expose-Worlds-Greatest-Secret/dp/1943957045

2. Wilcock, David. *Ascension Mysteries,* pg. 336.
https://www.amazon.com/Ascension-Mysteries-Revealing-Cosmic-Between-ebook/dp/B0191ZL2EC

Primaries
1. Koronowski, Ryan. "Debbie Wasserman Schultz Resigns from DNC in Wake of WikiLeaks Email Dump". https://thinkprogress.org/debbie-wasserman-schultz-resigns-from-dnc-in-wake-of-wikileaks-email-dump-d294bbdffb16
2. Powe, Alicia. "DNC: We Rigged Primaries. So what?" http://www.wnd.com/2017/05/dnc-we-rigged-primaries-so-what/
3. Sainato, Michael. "A Democrat Finally Admits DNC Rigged Primaries for Clinton". http://observer.com/2017/05/ro-khanna-admits-democratic-primares-rigged-for-hillary-clinton/
4. Sather, Jason. "...MSM Goes Full Anti-Hillary..." https://www.youtube.com/watch?v=En-VTreZMTs

Peaceful Revolution
1. Westall, Sarah, "Former Congresswoman & CIA Spy Call for Peaceful American Revolution". Galacticconnection.com
2. Our Revolution. www.ourrevolution.com

Iceland
1. Wikipedia
https://en.wikipedia.org/wiki/2009_Icelandic_financial_crisis_protests; Also see film by Michael Moore: "Where to Invade Next?".

Alternative News Sources: There are a great many alternative news sources on the internet that tend to share news the mainstream media does not—including much about disclosure about corruption and deception within the government. Some you may wish to explore are the following:
Operationdisclosure.com
Collective-evolution.com
Prepareforchange.net
Wakeupworld.com
Wakingtimes.com
Naturalnews.com
Mercola.com
Veteranstoday.com
Stillnessinthestorm.com
Zerohedge.com
Exopolitics.org

Chapter 5

Mind Control

As with everything else discussed so far, the belief that we are mind-controlled to some degree is probably not new to you. But perhaps you think you're free of most of that kind of control – that because you're smart and savvy about corruption and governmental lies, you're therefore a free thinker. In some ways, this is probably true – but you may not be totally aware of the wide-spread use of mind control tactics that occurs on multiple levels that cannot be escaped.

Mind control actually happens in many different areas of our lives – through the media, the entertainment industry, our educational systems, and our religious institutions. Also, very importantly, mind control operates quite effectively and insidiously through the common debunking of the truth about horrors the Cabal has created, by calling them "conspiracy theories".

So how can we see through and not be controlled by this manipulation and mind control so we can learn to somehow side-step it? Some of it is extremely subtle and most of it is so outrageous it is difficult to believe it's even happening. Just being aware of it, in all its forms, is the first step.

Manipulation through Movies, Books and Comics

As we will see in future chapters, many of the movies, books, and comics about hostile aliens and space craft have been based on information that has been purposely leaked to screen writers, authors and comic book creators by the Cabal with a specific purpose: to frighten us about possible alien attacks from outer space. Even though we may remind ourselves that what we're watching or reading is just fiction, the material nonetheless has a powerful impact on the subconscious mind and can create negative expectations about galactic contact.

Of course, there have also been the occasional films and TV shows about ETs that are benevolent and even heart-warming. But professionals in the field tell us that the ideas for these films too have been seeded by the Cabal working in the secret space programs as described in the next section of this book; and that these ideas have been given to screen writers with a secondary purpose: to hide the fact that there very definitely are those benevolent ETs both around and on the earth, by making them look fictional.

People running these secret space programs not only know about these positive ETs and work with them; they have also been working with the highly advanced technology the ETs have brought with them for decades now – technology that could have brought incredible benefit and freedom to the entire human race by now, but is being kept secret for the Cabal's own use and prosperity.

And so, by giving film makers and writers material for their creations, they are allowing this advanced technology to be shown, while making it look totally fictional. They do this so that, if whistle-blowers should decide to disclose the secrets from the programs, people will naturally disbelieve them. It would seem obvious that the supposed insiders just lifted their ideas from movies or from books they've read.

CIA and Pentagon Control of the Film Industry

Another way in which the Cabal works to control our minds through the movies and TV shows is through mandated CIA, Pentagon, and Department of Defense censorship within the Hollywood film industry. New documents leaked through WikiLeaks in July of 2017 revealed that nearly 1,800 movies and TV shows have borne the legal scrutiny of the Pentagon and CIA censors.

According to this evidence, if there is no seal of approval by these agencies, there is no production. In particular, in any film portraying the US military, if there are characters, action or dialogue that are not approved, the film-maker has to make changes to accommodate the military's protocols. To obtain full cooperation the producers have to sign contracts which lock them into using a military-approved version of the script. If they refuse, the government officials threaten to leave without granting their approval for the film.

Project MK Ultra

One of the most nefarious uses of mind control the government has employed is through what is known as "Project MK Ultra", sometimes referred to as the CIA's mind control program. Although it was officially halted in 1973, there are those who claim it is still being used.

MK Ultra is essentially a program of experiments performed on human subjects designed and illegally undertaken by the CIA. These experiments were initially intended to identify and develop drugs and procedures to be used in enemy interrogations and torture, in order to weaken the individual and force confessions through mind control.

According to a number of sources, and in particular an article on todayfoundout.com, "Project MK Ultra: One of the Most Shocking CIA Programs of All Time", beginning in the early 1950s, the operation illegally engaged unwitting U.S. and Canadian citizens as its test subjects. It employed numerous methods to manipulate people's mental states and alter brain functions, including the surreptitious administration of drugs and other chemicals, hypnosis, sensory deprivation, isolation and verbal abuse, as well as other forms of psychological torture.

News about the continuing use of MK Ultra techniques emerged recently when rock star Katy Perry began making strange, guttural noises before collapsing during a performance and had to be dragged off stage. Insiders commenting on this episode asserted that she was the latest MK Ultra-controlled victim to suffer a public meltdown.

A related story describes another program known as Monarch Mind Control, which employs a practice widely used by the Walt Disney Corporation and Teen Nick to sexualize and profit from young starlets.

According to an article, "Origins and Techniques of Monarch Mind Control" on the *Vigilant Citizen* website, Monarch Mind Control was developed in its current form by the CIA to subdue American citizens deemed "dangerous". It is currently being used by the Hollywood industrial complex to micro-manage child stars by taking advantage of their innocence and by appealing to the child's parents who commonly have a clear desire to make their child famous. The victims of this program are called "kittens" and the executives and managers who control them are known as "handlers".

Yet another story about the MK Ultra program has been released by Cathy O'Brien, in her article "Clintons, Haiti, Human Trafficking and Psych Warfare on Sexuality". In it she describes how the program has been used in Haiti. She states:

> "My experiences carrying out Black Ops in Haiti under MK Ultra mind control gave me deep insight into the plight of this traumatized nation. Haiti was being used as a testing ground for trauma-based mind control, multi-generational genetic alteration, infestation of AIDs, human trafficking, and an epicenter for CIA cocaine and heroin drug ops."

> "During my tenure under MK Ultra mind control carrying out White House/Pentagon level black ops for Shadow Government globalists like the Clintons in the 1980's, AIDs was deliberately introduced into Haiti through World Vision vaccines."

Media Control

A very important element of mind-control plays out through the mainstream media. Most people who only follow mainstream news have no idea that the news is being presented in a manner dictated by media corporations owned by the Cabal (which are named in Ashley Lutz's article, "These 6 Corporations Control 90% of the Media in America"). People are given only glimpses of real news that is not Cabal-spun. And they miss out on much news that is simply hidden or not reported, or they get a distorted version of it. In April 2017, a group called "Reporters without Borders" ranked the United States 43rd in the world in the category of Freedom of the Press.

It first became apparent that the Cabal had infiltrated the media when Anchorman Dan Rather on the CBS Sixty Minutes show attempted to reveal that George Bush's military records had been forged. Through a powerful attack on his producer, he was forced to retract what he had previously reported. He ended up quitting his position on the CBS News over this, very much disillusioned.

He stated that since he'd been in his position as the Sixty Minutes anchor, it had became apparent that his program could bring in a great deal of revenue, and that was the beginning of the end of the "Free Press" for CBS – and subsequently other successful mainstream news programs. Since then, all major media sources, all owned by Cabal-run corporations, have been offering only news that promotes what they want communicated to the public.

What has also been revealed on numerous sites and videos is that the media news is actually closely controlled by the CIA. Researcher Arjun Walia in "Declassified CIA Documents Show Agency's Control over Mainstream Media & Academia", reports that William Casey, former CIA Director, stated it well: "We shall know our disinformation program is complete when everything the American people believes is false."

Indeed, there are those who believe the CIA had actually penetrated the mainstream news as far back as the 1950s, when the CIA program known as "Operation Mockingbird" was launched. This was a CIA-based initiative to control the American public's opinions about what was going on in the US and in the world – not only through the media but also through the entertainment industry, as well.

A declassified document from the CIA archives in the form of a letter from a CIA task force addressed to the Director of the CIA details the close relationship that exists between the CIA and the mainstream media. The document states that the CIA "now has relationships with reporters from every major wire service, newspaper, newsweekly, and television network in the nation..."

Fake News War

Today we're being assaulted by what's become a "Fake News" war. Realizing at one point soon after the 2016 election that they were quickly losing viewers, the mainstream media began flinging mud at alternative news sources, calling numerous stories the alt news sites were showing "Fake News".

A mysterious group called "Prop or Not" seemed to appear out of nowhere, issuing a list of "fake news" sites, allegedly under "Russian control". Each link within the collection of blacklisted sites—up to 200 in total—began to be blocked or de-monetized by Facebook, Google, Apple, Snapchat and others. Since then, the alternative sites have been flinging the same "fake news" mud back at the mainstream sites. And very interestingly, we have seen certain mainstream news reports "correcting" certain "mistakes" they'd earlier made in their reporting.

However, when there's a war going on like this, there seems to be no way to know what is real and what is fake anymore, either on mainstream news or alternative news sources. All we can do is tune in and decide for ourselves what feels true to us. And hopefully not get caught up in the heated and divisive diatribes being hurled back and forth.

Conspiracy Theories

It gets even more serious than the matter of fake news, however. Thanks to the help of the CIA-controlled media, the shadow government has notoriously been able to commit crimes and blame them on patsies who take the fall. And anyone discovering the truth about this and trying to disseminate it is routinely ridiculed and labeled a "conspiracy theorist".

Most people are taught to blow off theories of government conspiracy and to ridicule anyone who believes in them. Through various methods of mind-control, the Cabal has taught us to label any proof of their own existence or their control as unfounded theories held by disgruntled, fringe individuals wanting to stir up controversy and unrest.

According to whistle blowers reporting to David Wilcock, the Cabal has three levels for dealing with people who have witnessed something the Cabal has tried to keep secret. Initially they send someone out to talk to the person, with the aim to stop them from disclosing what they've witnessed.

The first ploy they use is trying to convince the person that they didn't see what they actually saw – that they were hallucinating – or seeing what they "wanted to see". In one way or another, they attempt to explain away the person's experience.

If that ploy doesn't work and the person decides to continue disclosing what they've witnessed, the next step is to threaten the person and their family. And if that doesn't work, then it may be time to do away with them.

JFK Conspiracy Theory

One of the best examples of how this whole mind control strategy has played out in history is the JFK assassination. It's actually amazing how so many people to this day still believe the official story about a crazed killer named Lee Harvey Oswald shooting the president. They also believe the Warren Commission report as to how it all happened. Unbelievably, this report actually explained away what clearly appeared to be multiple bullets from different locations as the work of a single bullet that zigzagged around multiple times and hit several different people.

What's become clear to multiple researchers and authors of books on the subject (many which are listed on the Conscious Life News Website in "The 'Secret Society Speech' that Got JFK Killed") is that there were actually eight riflemen firing at JFK. It's well known where they were located and that many credible witnesses saw these men and gave precise descriptions of them. Even a cursory search online of the event reveals that Lee Harvey Oswald not only didn't act alone, he was more than likely not even one of the shooters. And – he was actually known to work for the CIA and drew a paycheck from the FBI.

Hundreds of other details have been revealed over the years that don't correlate with the official reports, including credible testimonies from doctors who treated JFK's body. And many more pointing to a small group of powerful men who had planned the event.

Just recently, a new video has released, "American Media and the Second Assassination of John F. Kennedy", and is currently the fifth most popular movie on Amazon. It's the story of Jim Garrison, who somehow managed to break through an almost complete media monopoly to reveal the truth of the JFK assassination by appearing on television shows such as *The Tonight Show* with Johnny Carson and *Real People.*

Indeed, all the evidence is there and has been for some time that there really was a conspiracy to kill JFK. Even the 1976 House Select Subcommittee on Assassinations found that the JFK assassination was probably a conspiracy. And yet, thanks to mind-control tactics used by the actual assassins, most people still remember Lee Harvey Oswald as Kennedy's murderer. More importantly, as always, nothing has been done to prosecute those actually responsible for this heinous crime.

Other Conspiracy Theories

Similarly, it's still believed by many that Martin Luther King, Jr. was assassinated by James Earl Ray. Yet there is so much evidence of Ray's innocence that not even the King family believes he was guilty. Similar fabricated stories were reported on the Robert Kennedy murder and on the attempted murder of Reagan. All with the same results.

The Cabal understands the human psyche well. Even when evidence comes out to the contrary, the first impact of the event causing a sense of horror and fear in the human mind is so powerful, that it's easier for people to take in explanations given to them about a "lone crazed killer" than to follow the evidence which eventually emerges about the situation.

False Flag Events

In case the term "false flag" is new to you, this refers to a covert operation that is designed to deceive in such a way that activities appear as though they are being carried out by entities, groups, or nations other than those who actually planned and executed them.

This concept first appeared on the scene in the last century in what's known as "Operation Gladio". The US and NATO allies used this operation in a decades-long campaign of false flag terror attacks directed by Western intelligence agencies that were responsible for the murder of hundreds of innocent civilians. Originally, it was set up after WWII using a clandestine group of operatives that were to be activated in the event of a Soviet invasion of Europe.

But, as described in a post on the Truth Move website, "Operation Gladio", the plan quickly evolved into a program of political repression and manipulation directed by NATO and the CIA. For decades, the Gladio group carried out widespread terrorist attacks, assassinations and electoral subversion in Western Europe that were portrayed to the public as Communist or Left Wing terror attacks.

Today these same kinds of attacks are generally blamed on a different "enemy" – Muslim terrorist groups. But whistle-blowers tell us these new enemy groups are still funded and trained by the CIA. Indeed, the Gladio concept has become an important element of the "War on Terror".

9/11 is probably the most famous of these false flag events. It's increasingly clear now that this horrific event was an inside job that had been explained away in a mass of lies. But evidently, many people still believe the story the public was given at the time, claiming that Muslim terrorists were responsible for the airplane downing of the twin towers and the Pentagon crash.

If by chance you still doubt that there's truth to the false flag explanation about 9/11, you'll find that there is a mountain of evidence that both 9/11 and George Bush's subsequent wars were planned long before 9/11 even happened. One single source to get the full story from is in Philip Marshall's book, *False Flag 911: How Bush, Cheney and the Saudis Created the Post-911 World.*

There are hundreds of other excellent books, articles, documentaries and videos that prove beyond a doubt that the government's version about what happened during the event was false. Indeed, documentaries have been shown around the world about this. Yet relatively few of these books or videos are available in book stores, video stores or libraries in the US. Sadly, in the rest of the world, Americans are known as the least educated population on the truth about 9/11.

False Flag operations since 9/11 have occurred in much the same way. There's the official story that the mainstream media has put out about who caused the terror attack and why. And there are the insiders and whistle-blowers who reveal the truth and are then labeled as "Conspiracy Theorists" to be dismissed.

More and more whistle-blowers are speaking out, however, in alternative news sources. One very credible insider, Robert David Steele, a former Marine Intelligence Officer and CIA Clandestine Officer, claims that most terrorists are false flag terrorists, or are created by US security services. In the US, "every single terrorist incident we have had has been a false flag, or has been an informant pushed on by the FBI."

Research will show you that many of the terrorist attacks in recent years in which people have reportedly been injured, murdered, and terrorized, have been false flag events. Manchester, Oklahoma City, Orlando, Boston, the Shoe Bomber, Charlottesville, Las Vegas. It becomes probable that these crimes have not been committed by those who are blamed or even by those "confessing" to them. There is always a connection leading back to the CIA or other intelligence agency.

Indeed, a well-documented post on www.washingtonsblog.com, "False Flag Terrorism Isn't a 'Theory'... It's ADMITTED and

Widespread", presents a long list of false flag events in which officials in the government that carried out the attacks have actually admitted to creating false flags, either orally, in writing, or through photographs or videos.

Author Paul C. Roberts concurs in "The War on Terror is the Hoax Foundation of the Police/Spy State", that the whole war on Terror is a hoax. The Powers that Be quite cleverly create havoc and terror in order to to keep us in fear, and therefore able to be manipulated. They then have a reason to create police state tactics that give them all the more control, while all the time acting as "saviors" to rescue us from the terrorists they themselves have created.

And of course, the CIA-controlled mainstream news sources jump on board, doing their part to keep the terror going. In fact, they sometimes more than add to the lies given by official sources – they actually at times create lies themselves.

A number of mainstream reporters have been caught on videos that clearly show that people in so-called protests or riots are actually hired actors. These actors have been noted to be at several different terror attacks and protest scenes, saying the same things at each event. In fact, ads for "crisis actors" have been spotted in a number of magazines and internet sites, both in the US and Canada.

And, really unbelievably, as Richard Spilette describes in his post, "CNN reporter is caught up in 'fake news' row after being accused of 'setting up' a Muslim counter-terror protest", sometimes videos of certain terror attacks were actually taken *before* an event even happened. It's also been noted that a post has appeared on Wikipedia with a description of a terror attack with a prescribed spin on it, even before the event actually occurred.

In general, it's important to keep in mind when considering terror attacks that the Cabal's purpose above all is to keep us both uninformed and afraid, and therefore amenable to their control tactics. Additionally, they know well how to teach us to respect and obey "authority" – and to rely on authority figures. So when they create terror events, they can then step in with police state tactics to "save" us. In other words, they create the problem, and then they offer the solution so that we will give up our autonomy to them for rescuing us and continuing to keep us safe.

Religious Control

Another way the Cabal has exercised mind-control throughout the centuries is through infiltrating religions and creating dogma and scriptures that have suited their own purposes. In particular, this has happened dramatically within the Catholic Church. It's common knowledge by certain theologians that the Christian Bible was greatly edited and altered in the fourth century by design.

This process omitted all references to reincarnation and also added passages to instill fear and induce obedience to the Church. In addition, by eliminating certain gospels, some of the most important teachings of Jesus, including those about the role of women in the early church, became unavailable. It's probable these passages were too threatening to the control of the male church hierarchy.

I am not going into detail here about the corruption within the Vatican that is now being revealed. You can do your own research if you wish to know what is involved. Let me only say that truly dark rituals evidently still take place across the world by those Cabal members connected to the Vatican – and also perhaps even within the walls of the Holy City itself.

Educational Control

As we've seen in Chapter 4, the actual history of the US has not been taught in American classrooms. Not only have students been taught the history written by the victors, which is greatly skewed to begin with; they've also been taught erroneous information and history with many gaps in it.

Other ways in which our schools prepare children for adulthood also reflect the agenda of the Cabal to keep them ignorant – and, very importantly, not well prepared to think for themselves. As we all know, the approach is generally to get them to digest tons of information which they then are required to regurgitate on standardized tests.

This approach tends to squash any original thinking and doesn't consider the different talents, inherent wisdom, or particular inclinations of individual students. And it most definitely prepares children to be adults who are deferential toward authority – who then become subjects to be easily controlled.

There are a number of people at this point who are intent on turning around this educational approach in schools featuring innovative ways of teaching and drawing from the children themselves what they wish to learn. Finland is a world leader in proving the success of this approach. But in the US, schools like this are generally private and cost a lot to attend.

However, if you search, you can find there is some progress a few US public schools are making in at least treating children with respect. In certain Baltimore schools, for example, children who misbehave are no longer being sent to the Principal's office to be punished. They are sent instead to the "Mindful Moment Room".

This is a room equipped with bean bags and dim lighting. The children sent there are taken through calming exercises with trained staff, including instruction in breathing exercises and mindfulness meditation. After twenty minutes in this room, the children are sent back to rejoin their classmates. The program reports great success in eliminating disciplinary problems and emotional outbursts among the children.

The progress is slow, but little by little, our schools are waking up.

* * *

If you've been reading these beginning chapters one after the other, you may be feeling the weight of contemplating all the control and manipulation the Cabal exercises over us. It can be overwhelming. If so, see if you can feel the outrage and grief that may arise with this – and then do your best to let these feelings go.

Remember that there is much progress, still behind the scenes at this point, in putting an end to all of it, once and for all. We are assured, as you'll see in Chapter 14, that at some point in the not too distant future, we will see the fall of the Cabal and be freed from their control.

But meanwhile, just to get the full picture, let's look at one more important area in which the Cabal plays a part in making our lives difficult—that of our health.

Mind Control – References

Movies, Books & Comics
1. Editor, Event Chronicle. "FOIA Docs Show CIA/Pentagon Made 1,800 Movies, TV Shows to Make America Love War". http://www.theeventchronicle.com/uncategorized/foia-docs-show-ciapentagon-made-1800-movies-tv-shows-make-america-love-war/
2. Secker, Don. Documents expose how Hollywood promotes war on behalf of the Pentagon, CIA and NSA". https://medium.com/insurge-intelligence/exclusive-documents-expose-direct-us-military-intelligence-influence-on-1-800-movies-and-tv-shows-36433107c307
3. Wilcock, David. *Ascension Mysteries,* pg. 344. https://www.amazon.com/s/ref=nb_sb_noss_1?url=search-alias%3Dstripbooks&field-keywords=david+wilcock

Monarch Mind Control
1. Editor, *The Vigilant Citizen.* "Origins and Techniques of Monarch Mind Control". https://vigilantcitizen.com/hidden-knowledge/origins-and-techniques-of-monarch-mind-control/
2. Editor, *Collective Evolution.* "Another Side of The Music Industry: Monarch Mind Control". http://www.collective-evolution.com/2013/10/08/monarch-mind-control-popular-music/

Project MK Ultra
1. O'Brien, Cathy. "Cathy O'Brien: Ex-Illuminati Mind Control Victim". https://www.youtube.com/watch?v=FvEBmEo4IA0
2. Melissa. "Project Mkultra: One of the Most Shocking CIA Programs of All Time". http://gizmodo.com/project-mkultra-one-of-the-most-shocking-cia-programs-1370236359

Media Control
1. Duclos, Susan. "Media Blackout on Four Major Bombshells that Destroy the Preferred MSM Narrative". http://www.theeventchronicle.com/news/north-america/media-blackout-four-major-bombshells-destroy-msm-preferred-narrative/
2. Kurtz, Howard. "Dan Rather to Step Down at CBS". http://www.washingtonpost.com/wp-dyn/articles/A7313-2004Nov23.html
Also see film entitled "Truth" with Robert Redford and Cate Blanchett.
3. Lutz, Ashley. "These 6 Corporations Control 90% of the Media in America." http://www.businessinsider.com/these-6-corporations-control-90-of-the-media-in-america-2012-6
4. McShay, Patrick J. "Kennedy, Lennon, Reagan, and 9/11 -- The Bush Connection". http://operationdisclosure.blogspot.com/2017/05/kennedy-lennon-reagan-and-911-bush.html

5. Sather, Jason. "...MSM Goes Full Anti-Hillary..."
https://www.youtube.com/watch?v=En-VTreZMTs
6. Walia, Arjun. "Declassified CIA Documents Show Agency's Control Over Mainstream Media & Academia". http://www.collective-evolution.com/2017/05/11/declassified-cia-documents-shows-agencies-control-over-mainstream-media-academia/

Operation Mockingbird
1. "Operation Mockingbird" CIA Secret Campaign 1950's"
https://www.youtube.com/watch?v=a9Ac4nSjSlc
2. St. Clair, Jeffrey. "The CIA and the Press: When the Washington Post Ran the CIA's Propaganda Network".
https://www.counterpunch.org/2016/11/30/the-cia-and-the-press-when-the-washington-post-ran-the-cias-propaganda-network/

Fake News
Anti-Media News Desk. "Fake News Exposed: New York Times Finally Corrects Bogus Claim That Iran 'Sponsored' 9/11 Attacks".
http://theantimedia.org/new-york-times-iran-sponsored-911/

Conspiracy Theories
1. "American Media & The Second Assassination of John F. Kennedy"
http://www.imdb.com/title/tt6670304/plotsummary?ref_=tt_ov_pl
2. "Boom: Charlottesville Police Officer Tells All."
https://www.youtube.com/watch?v=bFNOfG7Zbzc
3. Conscious Life News Website. "The 'Secret Society Speech' that Got JFK Killed".
http://consciouslifenews.com/secret-society-speech-jfk-killed/1178286/
4. DeHaven-Smith, Lance. *Conspiracy Theory in America.*
https://utpress.utexas.edu/books/dehcon
5. Hodges, Dave. "JFK, RFK & MLK Were All Killed by the Same Forces".
http://www.thecommonsenseshow.com/2013/11/17/jfk-rfk-mlk-were-all-killed-by-the-same-forces/
6. "JFK to 9/11: Everything is a Rich Man's Trick".
https://www.youtube.com/watch?v=U1Qt6a-vaNM&t=883s
7. Preston, James. "The Coming Shift to Cosmic Fascism (Part II)".
http://www.veteranstoday.com/2017/05/21/the-coming-shift-to-cosmic-fascism-part-ii/
8. "The 'Secret Society' Speech That Got JFK Killed".
http://www.thecommonsenseshow.com/2013/11/17/jfk-rfk-mlk-were-all-killed-by-the-same-forces/
9. Spilette, Richard. "CNN reporter is caught up in 'fake news' row after being accused of 'setting up' a Muslim counter-terror protest".
http://www.dailymail.co.uk/news/article-4573882/Fake-news-row-Muslim-protesters-TV-crews.html

10. Truth Move website. "Operation Gladio".
http://www.truthmove.org/content/operation-gladio/
11. Wilcock, David. *Ascension Mysteries,* pg. 354.
https://www.amazon.com/Ascension-Mysteries-Revealing-Cosmic-Between-ebook/dp/B0191ZL2EC

False Flags

1. Barrett, Kevin. "False Flag Weekly News, Veterans Today".
http://noliesradio.org/archives/category/archived-shows/false-flag-weekly-news
2. Blevins, Rachel. "CNN Actually Admits They Published Fake News".
http://thefreethoughtproject.com/cnn-published-fake-news-comey/
3. Dolan, Richard. "Introducing False Flags".
https://www.gaia.com/video/introducing-false-flags?fullplayer=feature
4. Ganser, Daniel. *NATO's Secret Armies: Operation Gladio and Terrorism in Western Europe.*
5. Heyes, JD. "CNN, AP Caught Staging Fake News Protest in London."
http://www.stillnessinthestorm.com/2017/06/cnn-ap-caught-staging-fake-news-protest-in-london-to-help-cover-up-radical-terrorism-attack.html?utm_source=feedburner&utm_medium=email&utm_campaign=Feed%3A+StillnessInTheStormBlog+%28Stillness+in+the+Storm+Blog%29
6. Marshall, Philip. *False Flag 911: How Bush, Cheney and the Saudis Created the Post-911 World.* https://www.amazon.com/False-Flag-911-Created-Post-911/dp/1439202648
7. McShay, Patrick J. Operation Gladio And The False Flag Muslim Terror Hoax
https://www.thetruthseeker.co.uk/?p=152946
8. Roberts, Paul Craig. "The "War On Terror" Is The Hoax Foundation Of The Police/Spy State"
http://www.paulcraigroberts.org/2015/11/05/the-war-on-terror-is-the-hoax-foundation-of-the-policespy-state-paul-craig-roberts/
9. WashingtonsBlog. "False Flag Terrorism Isn't a "Theory" ... It's ADMITTED and Widespread".
http://www.washingtonsblog.com/2017/07/ff.html

Religious Control

1. "Integrating the Dark and the Light: Remembering Evolution"
http://integratingdarkandlight.com/cabals-web-of-control/
2. James, Preston. "35 Things the Ruling Cabal Does Not Want You to Know" http://www.veteranstoday.com/2013/09/02/35-things-the-ruling-cabal-does-not-want-you-to-know/

Educational Control
1. Livergood, Norman D. The Destruction of American Education And What We Must Do about It. http://www.hermes-press.com/education_index.htm
2. Logue, Gretchen. No Wonder the Education Cabal is Afraid of Homeschooling Families. They Aren't Accountable to the Government & NGOs. http://missourieducationwatchdog.com/no-wonder-the-education-cabal-is-afraid-of-homeschooling-families-they-arent-accountable-to-the-government-ngos/
3. Welsh, Teresa. "Schools Replace Punishment with Meditation". http://www.miamiherald.com/news/nation-world/national/article103688417.html

Military Intelligence Complex
Editor, The Event Chronicle. "20 Ex-Intelligence Agents Expose the Military Intelligence Complex". http://www.theeventchronicle.com/study/20-ex-intelligence-agents-expose-military-intelligence-complex-recommended/

Chapter 6

Health Control

Most of what I present in this chapter is probably not new to you. But again, it's important to see all of it together to recognize the sheer bulk of the number of threats that exist in our world to our health and physical well-being. When you really step back and take it all in, you can see this is not just due to corporate greed perpetrated by people who are out to make a buck in any way they can—although that of course also plays a part.

As I've said, part of the Cabal's control tactics is to keep us not only poor, dumbed down, powerless, fearful and working at jobs that are deadening – but also unhealthy and weak. And they have designed a large variety of ways in which to keep us in deteriorating health.

Food Contamination

For example, we know that, unless we buy organic, non-GMO, preservative-free foods, we're going to be ingesting harmful chemicals into our bodies of one kind or another. Even then, we can't always be sure. Certain companies make claims that turn out not to be true, or we find that they've exchanged one dangerous chemical for another.

This has been true for so long, it's just something we tend to accept as how the world works these days. But if you stop to think about it, simply the fact that foods that are so available to us are actually dangerous for us has to give you pause. Is it just "normal" corporate greed and dishonesty that have created this situation – or is there something else much more nefarious occurring?

David Wilcock reports insider information that tells us that food has actually been intentionally "weaponized" in different ways since the 1970s. For example, a protein called gliadin was intentionally added to wheat at some point – a substance that mimics the hormone the thyroid needs – so that when ingested, the gliadin locks onto the thyroid, causing a sensation of on-going hunger.

We tend to think that it's just the sugar in wheat products that makes them addictive, but it's obviously not just that. And people wonder why obesity in the Western world has become so pervasive. To really get the picture about the damage to human health through the foods that are available to us, see "Fed Up", an online video written and produced by Stephanie Soechtig.

Poisoned Water

And then there's our water. As with food, we know that tap water is not truly safe to drink. Effective filtering systems tend be expensive, so many people turn to bottled water – usually unaware that the plastic most bottled water comes in is full of a poisonous compound, BPA. And even many of those companies now claiming their bottles are "BPA-Free" are instead using BPA substitutes, some of which have been tested to be even more harmful to the human body than BPA.

But how can most people realistically avoid drinking tap water altogether? It's difficult, at best. And so, naturally, all that has been put into our "safe" water supply is ingested. And one of the most harmful substances in our water in the US is fluoride.

In this country, water fluoridation has been widespread for the last 75 years. Despite the fact that clear-cut evidence suggests consuming the fluoride added to drinking water is dangerous to human health and does nothing to protect teeth from cavities, governments and protective agencies have done nothing to stop the practice of adding fluoride to city water systems.

In doing so, among other things, they ignore the fact that in the US, 57 percent of youth between ages of 6 and 19 years have dental fluorosis ("mottled enamel"), characterized by hypomineralization of the tooth enamel. In addition, another study shows fluoride's potential to lower IQ in children.

There are now over 100 animal studies and over 50 human studies proving fluoride's neurotoxicity. In fact, according to the world's oldest and most prestigious medical journal, *Lancet*, fluoride is classified in the same category as arsenic, lead and mercury. And yet, it continues to be recommended by nearly all public health and academic institutions and dentists.

Metaphysical sources describe how fluoride actually acts to block the activity of the pineal gland, dulling down the ability of a person to be aware of higher spiritual energies.

Big Pharma Contaminating Waters

Another way in which our water is no longer safe is the incredible amount of toxic drugs that have found their way into our water supply. Drugs from pharmaceutical companies contaminate nearly all the water in America with chemicals that alter biology, fertility and even gender expression.

Although some sources report that trace amounts of a great number of different pharmaceuticals have been found in America's drinking water, even the mainstream journal *Scientific American* reports that up to fourteen different pharmaceuticals have been found. Two of the most concerning drugs are pharmaceutical amphetamines and methamphetamines. Researchers have found these two drugs with varying levels of concentration in their samples at all six sites they studied. As you may know, amphetamines are used in drugs for ADHD. As someone quipped, "Need your ADHD medicine? Just take a sip of tap water."

Other medications that flood our waters are pain medication, antidepressants and cholesterol-lowering statins. Birth control pills and other hormone supplements also appear, many of which do not break down easily.

Fracking

There are huge concerns associated with natural gas and shale gas extraction, including hydraulic fracturing, known as "fracking". The first concern is the amount of water needed in the fracking process. It's been figured that the amount of water used in just one fracture could actually supply a household of four with water for 51 years. But an even worse result of fracking is the contamination of underground and surface waters resulting from spills, faulty well construction, or other means.

Many studies have detailed the contaminants that have entered the waters through nearby fracking activities. One connected the death of more than 100 cattle to exposure to fracking fluids. Another found methane concentrations 17 times higher in waters connected to fracking. And yet another found one million pounds of chemicals used at a single well site. In addition, it has been found that there may be a strong connection between fracking and local earthquakes.

In 2015, the administration issued a long-awaited study of the fracking technique that confirmed that fracking "led to impacts on drinking water resources, including contamination of drinking water wells". And yet, two years later, the practice of fracking continues.

Oil Spills

It's always horrific to hear about oil spills in our oceans and the damage done to the environment after each one. And occasionally, we may hear that the chemicals in the oceans at some point have begun affecting humans who live near these spills. But often other more engaging news is reported, and the stories of the oil spills have moved to the background of everyone's awareness.

And yet the spills and the health dangers they cause continue. When people have direct exposure to oil spills, just breathing the contaminated air is harmful. Oil has many volatile compounds which are emitted as gases, and the air becomes contaminated with those products or vapors. Even when odors are not present, a health risk may exist for nearby residents who are exposed for a long time. If the oil is absorbed by skin – say by someone walking on a beach or swimming in waters nearby – it can be absorbed through the skin into the body.

The other way petroleum products can enter our bodies from oil spills is through eating contaminated food. Some oil compounds bioaccumulate in living organisms and may become more concentrated along the food chain.

Chemtrails

You've probably heard about chemtrails not being good for our health – but you may not realize just how harmful these toxic aerosols are or that they are part of the over-arching plan to keep us in weakened health. Chemtrails are very deliberately sprayed into the upper atmosphere so that the particles from the sprays fall, usually without notice, to the ground where they enter our soil, water and respiratory systems.

Scientists have been testing soil and water that have received this fallout, and the results are shocking: toxic aluminum, barium and other elements have been found to be thousands of times higher than US acceptable levels. These high levels lead to very irregular, extremely acidic Ph levels in the soil and water, which can be deadly to ecological life systems, including our own.

Electromagnetic Radiation

Most people have no idea that the electromagnetic radiation emanating from our cell phones, computers, WiFi and cell towers is actually not safe for us. Younger generations have grown up in our EMF-saturated environment and can't remember a time when it wasn't present. Also the radiation is invisible, so the assumption is that it must be okay for us.

Unfortunately, there are studies telling us that cell phones and WiFi are safe – or at least they claim there is no evidence that they are unsafe. However, if you locate the funding source for most of these studies, you'll find that the corporations funding them were the very ones which produce cell phones and wireless devices.

In addition, there is now an abundance of independent, peer-reviewed studies from all over the world that have conclusively linked EMF exposure with a wide variety of adverse health effects and serious diseases. Among other things, exposure to electromagnetic radiation greatly stresses the immune system, gradually wearing it down over time. This in turn causes cellular malfunctioning, breaks DNA strands, and creates stress hormones.

Symptoms people experience with EMF exposure vary, depending on each body's genetic vulnerabilities. But some of the more common symptoms include headaches, fatigue, sleep disturbances, chronic colds and flus, and mood disturbances.

According to certain research studies, these symptoms may eventually develop into more serious disorders and diseases, such as Alzheimer's or high blood pressure – as well as a number of other immune-deficiency diseases such as Lyme disease or fibromyalgia. And, very importantly, in children radiation exposure has been clearly correlated with autism, ADHD, and asthma.

HAARP

HAARP (High Frequency Active Auroral Research Program) is a critically important U.S. military defense program which has generated quite a bit of controversy over the years. Some respected researchers allege that secret electromagnetic warfare capabilities of HAARP are designed to forward the US military's stated goal of achieving full-spectrum dominance by the year 2020.

In addition, HAARP has been using technology for a number of decades for weather modification, causing earthquakes and tsunamis in order to disrupt global communication systems. It has also been used to create droughts and storms. There is documentation revealing that weather modification has further been used as warfare by the US since the 1940s.

Much of this program has remained secret for quite some time. Of course, the reason given behind the secrecy is "national security" – the standard explanation for nefarious governmental activities that are hidden from us. But the scary thing to contemplate is if the military secretly developed a weapon over half a century ago which could cause a tsunami, what kind of advanced deadly weapons might be available now?

There is much evidence that the severe hurricanes that occurred in late 2017 were engineered and manipulated by technology. Many videos online by scientists, engineers and investigative reporters describe how the storms, although probably not totally manufactured, were nonetheless enhanced, "driven", and "parked" by artificial forces. In essence, the Cabal was able to turn what is a natural, cyclical event on earth--a "purification process" of earth changes and global warming the planet goes through regularly--into a human disaster.

Big Pharma Pushing Pills

Reading statistics about prescription drugs can be a bit scary. Two of the lesser known facts about prescription drugs are, first, that new drugs have a one in five chance of causing serious reactions, even after being approved. And secondly, that prescription drugs are the fourth leading cause of death in the US. And this is not about overdosing or misprescribing. These are drugs that are deemed safe and properly prescribed to patients who simply have an adverse reaction to them.

Then there are the out-and-out lies that Big Pharma tells us. Like how cancer cannot be cured without chemotherapy or radiation and the associated drugs. The statistics on people going through chemo versus those who choose not to are staggering: those who go the chemo route have less chance of extending their lives than those choosing to do nothing. One study even proved that chemo is ineffective more than 97% of the time.

Or how about the claim that ADHD medication is "safer than aspirin" and can "increase kids' test scores"? As Kaylee Brown points out in "10 Colossal False Health Claims Made by Big Pharma & Mainstream Media", pharmaceutical companies pay doctors and researchers to overstate the dangers of ADHD and the benefits of taking their drugs, while understating the negative side effects. These drugs can have significant side effects and are actually considered to be within the same class as morphine and oxycodone due to their high risk of abuse and addiction.

Flu shots are another example. We hear from doctors that these shots are necessary and are 100% effective. This is often considered the biggest joke by many in the know within the medical industry. They consist of terrible ingredients, including formaldehyde and mercury – two powerful neurotoxins. Even according to a report by the Center for Disease Control, it's clear that flu shots only work approximately 50% of the time. And then there's the study published in the *International Journal of Medicine* revealing that flu vaccines can result in inflammatory cardiovascular changes indicative of increased risk for serious heart-related diseases, such as heart attacks.

Another little known fact is noted by author Melody Petersen in her book, *Our Daily Meds*. She states that 100,000 Americans die each year from prescription drugs. That is 270 a day—or more than twice as many who are killed in car accidents each day. But then, many of the deaths due to car accidents include those that are due to prescription-drugged drivers, so the statistics of drug-induced deaths are even more staggering. And these numbers nearly doubled between 2005 and 2015.

Vaccinations

Flu vaccinations are voluntary. But how about the vaccinations every child must now get in certain school systems before they can attend school? This is difficult for parents to oppose, as both pharmaceutical companies and government organizations support an agenda in which vaccinations are promoted as an essential tool to prevent disease. Dr. Joseph Mercola reports that medical practitioners are rewarded for high vaccination rates. Indeed, doctors are often pressured to vaccinate patients or face negative professional and financial consequences.

And yet, there is no proof showing that vaccinated children are healthier than unvaccinated children. The Center for Disease Control and Prevention (CDC), taking the stance that the science is settled, states that to do such a study would be "immoral", as it would withhold "life-saving" preventatives from the population. Yet there is a recent study which showed that unvaccinated kids are actually healthier than vaccinated ones.

It seems that the truly "immoral" thing to do would be for the CDC to deny, for instance, that there is a vaccine-autism link. This link has been proven numerous times. It's not just a theory dreamt up by concerned parents; it surfaced when scientists found that link. A study published by Dr. Brian A. Hooker, a previous CDC scientist, in the peer-reviewed journal *Translational Neuro-degeneration,* found up to a 340% increased risk of autism in African American boys receiving the Measles-mumps-rubella vaccine.

And autism isn't the only serious effect of vaccines. Other adverse events reported during post-approval use of the Tripedia vaccine include SIDS, anaphylactic reaction, cellulitis, convulsion/ grand mal convulsion and a variety of other equally awful conditions.

The Healthcare Racket

On top of facing all this in our interactions with the medical professions, we also have to deal with the issue of having healthcare insurance so that we can even afford to get medical treatment, should we need it. The federal government's role in providing healthcare to Americans is one of the most fraught subjects in today's politics.

Although all other first-world countries have been successful in creating effective and affordable healthcare for their citizens, the US remains so far behind in this endeavor, it is difficult to believe that the difficulties the government seems unable to resolve are not purposely contrived.

One of the main reasons, of course, is the role that Big Pharma plays in the decisions policy makers come to in their efforts to create a healthcare plan that all can agree on. Big Pharma is not only extremely powerful; it is also, like all other similar conglomerates in the US, run by the deep state factions that put profit and business interests ahead of patients' lives and well-being.

Population Control

It may be a stretch to think in terms of people purposely trying to keep the human population numbers under control, but there are those, such as the editor of the Health Freedom Alliance website, who present evidence that this is also part of the plan of the Elite – to not only keep humanity as unhealthy and weak as possible, but also to eliminate large groups of people through methods of population control.

We have already reviewed above many of the methods that serve to make people sick. And it's easy to find statistics that more and more people these days are ill, often on a chronic basis. Indeed, contemporary humanity is quite clearly facing an unprecedented crisis of deteriorating health. But what's important to be aware of according to the Health Freedom Alliance is that the various health conditions that increasingly plague us appear to be *intentionally* inflicted as part of a covert effort to reduce the world's population.

According to this source, there are a number of common health symptoms that point to a sinister, "slow kill" agenda that's been designed to quietly cull the masses without overt fanfare. These include such health problems as gut and digestion issues, chronic fatigue and low energy, obesity, diabetes, brain fog, chronic inflammation, allergies and chemical imbalances. Health practitioners everywhere in the US report that they deal with increasing numbers of patients with these conditions.

It gets even more concerning when you read that the UN has a plan to halt population growth. According to Christina Sarich, staff writer for *Waking Times,* the United Nations has actually been planning a depopulation agenda for decades. Recently the UN's Executive Secretary of the Framework Convention on Climate Change, Christiana Figueres, clearly stated that depopulation is part of the "green" agenda to "save the planet from global warming": "We all know, we expect 9 billion by 2050, so yes obviously less people would exert less pressure on the natural resources."

About the argument of "overpopulation": This is often used by those wanting an excuse to cull the masses. Overpopulation describes a situation where the *number of people* exhausts the resources in a *closed environment* such that it can no longer support that population.

The current closed environment relies on keeping people in poverty, using fossil fuels, and by dumping every toxic poison and chemical possible where people must live, wash, breathe, and reproduce. In this environment, yes, the argument may hold.

But as we know, these conditions have been foisted upon us by those in power – and aren't necessary. This argument also simply blames people's *numbers* for the problems we collectively face instead of holding individuals and groups (like corporations who largely run the UN) accountable for their actions.

Then there's the argument that "We Don't Have Enough Food". This comes from a notorious "over-population" man, Thomas Malthus. He believed in the 1800s that the world was doomed if it out-populated its food sources.

Again, this might sound like a reasonable argument. However, there are numerous scholarly articles proving that we waste several hundreds of tons of food every year. According to a recent report by the World Resources Institute (WRI), about one-third of all food produced worldwide, worth around US$1 trillion, gets lost or wasted in food production and consumption systems.

The same is true of the "We don't have enough water" myth. Of course, if water continues to be privatized and made a commodity, then there certainly isn't enough. As with food production, it's about utilizing resources effectively. There is plenty of water in the world in oceans – as well as technology to desalinate it very cost-effectively. So this is obviously a humanitarian issue, not an overpopulation one.

If you do research more deeply on this issue, you'll find even more sinister information about the depopulation agenda that the Powers That Be have. You will see that we face more "pandemics" than ever, and the fertility rates of the poorest nations are in decline.

Kevin Galalae's paper, "Turning Nature against Man: The Role of Pandemics Vaccines and Genetics in the UN's Plan to Halt Population Growth," shows fertility charts that are alarming.

Pregnant women who are directed to take H1N1 influenza vaccines are just the very scary beginning.

If you add to these charts the Zika virus, the bird flu and other pandemics that were evidently manufactured – on top of all the other issues outlined in this chapter – you begin to really comprehend the sinister aspects of the population control agenda.

Advanced Health Technology Being Held Back

As you're probably aware, a number of scientists have discovered cures for diseases like cancer; but, thanks to Big Pharma, they've been labeled quacks and have often had their licenses to practice medicine in the US revoked.

But also, perhaps even more important to understand, is that the Cabal has been holding back very advanced health technology given to them by ETs years ago that would not only cure diseases but also add healthy years to people's lifetimes. We'll visit this information in future chapters.

Deaths of Holistic Doctors

Perhaps one of the most frightening signs of the Cabal's control – although it could perhaps be a sign of their panic about losing control – is that in the last year or so, there have been a number of holistic doctors who have been murdered. At first, it seemed a coincidence that a few holistic doctors were dying, some of them made to look like suicides, some out-and-out murders, and some "unexplainable" deaths.

But then people started taking note of how the numbers of these doctors' deaths were increasing and they began keeping count. As of March 2016, sixty had been counted. Elizabeth Erin, wife of the well-known Dr. Mercola, is one who's been watching closely (for obvious reasons). But visionary author and film maker Foster Gamble has too. What is especially sad, Erin states, is that "these healers – some of whom were best-selling authors – were kind, caring people who have left this world a better place".

The Tide is Turning

As depressing as it may be to consider all the ways in which the Cabal controls our attempts to stay healthy, it's important to focus on signs that things are already changing, even on the level of governmental decisions. For example, in September 2014, the Indian Government launched their revolutionary "Rastriya Krishi Vikas Yojana" (National Agriculture Development Program) as a way to encourage organic farming, and decrease dependence on chemical agents. In January 2015, the Indian state of Sikkim was declared the country's first one hundred percent organic state. There are many other stories out there like this that are very encouraging.

The tide is turning—we just need to keep our focus on that, as we continue to navigate our way through the turbulent waters of the transition currently taking place.

HEALTH CONTROL REFERENCES

Food
1. Batts, Vicki. "Indian State will Pay Farmers to go 100% Organic".
http://www.stillnessinthestorm.com/2017/06/indian-state-will-pay-farmers-to-go-100-organic-and-gmo-free.html#more
2. Soechtig, Stephanie."Fed Up".
https://www.youtube.com/watch?v=1HI_woehm0Q
3. Wilcock, David. "Weaponized Wheat Since '60s".
https://www.youtube.com/watch?v=QO3mT2PQn0w

Fluoride
1. Cooper, Stuart. "Unprecedented Lawsuit Could End Water Fluoridation in US Based on Neurotoxicity Studies".
http://articles.mercola.com/sites/articles/archive/2017/06/13/ban-artificial-water-fluoridation.aspx
2. Froelich, Amanda. "6 ways to detox fluoride, a known neurotoxin, from your body"
http://www.theeventchronicle.com/health/6-ways-detox-fluoride-known-neurotoxin-body/
3. Mercola, Joseph. "Fluoridated Water Destroys Brain and Teeth".
http://articles.mercola.com/sites/articles/archive/2017/05/23/fluorida ted-water-destroys-brain-teeth.aspx

BPA
1. Abrams, Lindsey. "Study: BPA alternative may be worse than the harmful chemical it replaced".
http://www.salon.com/2015/01/13/study_finds_bpa_alternative_may_b e_worse_than_bpa_itself/
2. Bilbrey, Jenna. "BPA-Free Plastic Containers May Be Just as Hazardous"
https://www.scientificamerican.com/article/bpa-free-plastic-containers-may-be-just-as-hazardous/

Fracking
1. Ohio Environmental Council. "Fracking Impacts: Water Quality".
http://www.theoec.org/campaign/fracking-impacts-water-quality
2. JH. "The Link Between Fracking and Earthquakes Is Becoming Clearer".
https://www.the-american-interest.com/2017/06/25/the-link-between-fracking-earthquakes/

Oil Spills
Environmental Pollution Centers. "Oil Spills' Effects on Human Life".
https://www.environmentalpollutioncenters.org/oil-spill/humans/

Chemtrails
Phillipson, Troy. "Chemtrails Pose Serious and Increasing Health Risks to U.S. Citizens". http://www.geoengineeringwatch.org/chemtrails-pose-serious-and-increasing-health-risks-to-u-s-citizens/

EMFs
Mercola, Joseph. "EMF Articles". http://emf.mercola.com/

HAARP
1. Burks, Fred. "HAARP: Secret Weapon Used For Weather Modification, Electromagnetic Warfare". http://www.globalresearch.ca/haarp-secret-weapon-used-for-weather-modification-electromagnetic-warfare/20407
2. "Hurricane Harvey & the Weather Terrorists from Land, Sea and Air". https://www.youtube.com/watch?v=WzHSuT1z-I4&t=1016s

Big Pharma
1. Bigger, Cameron S. "4 Popular Companies Who Own the Medical Treatments For the Diseases Their Products Cause" http://www.wakingtimes.com/2017/08/15/4-popular-companies-medical-treatments-diseases-products-cause/
2. Brown, Kalee. "10 Colossal False Health Claims Made By Big Pharma & Mainstream Media". http://www.collective-evolution.com/2017/06/09/10-colossal-false-health-claims-made-by-big-pharma-mainstream media/?utm_source=feedburner&utm_medium=email&utm_campaign=Feed%3A+Collective-evolution+%28Collective+Evolution%29
3. Perdomo, Daniella. "100,000 Americans Die Each Year from Prescription Drugs, While Pharma Companies Get Rich" http://www.alternet.org/story/147318/100%2C000_americans_die_each_year_from_prescription_drugs%2C_while_pharma_companies_get_rich
4. Samuelson, D. "Big Pharma is contaminating nearly all the Water in America with Toxic drugs that alter Biology, Fertility and Even Gender Expression". http://www.naturalnews.com/2017-05-23-big-pharma-is-contaminating-nearly-all-the-water-in-america-with-toxic-drugs-that-alter-biology-fertility-and-even-gender-expression.html
5. Watson, Tracey. "Driving While Medicated" now a greater danger to society than driving drunk: Crashes from prescription meds up 100% in past decade". http://www.naturalnews.com/2017-06-04-driving-while-medicated-now-a-greater-danger-to-society-than-driving-drunk-crashes-from-prescription-meds-up-100-in-past-decade.html

Vaccines

1. Center for Disease Control. "Vaccine Effectiveness - How Well Does the Flu Vaccine Work?"
https://www.cdc.gov/flu/about/qa/vaccineeffect.htm
2. Frompovich, Catherine J. "FDA Announces That DTap Vaccine Can Cause Autism".
http://www.activistpost.com/2016/04/vaccine-maker-admits-on-fda-website-dtap-vaccine-causes-autism.html
3. Goldstein, Michelle. "How Do US Vaccine Rates, Policies and Children's Health Compare to Other Countries?"
http://www.theeventchronicle.com/health/us-vaccine-rates-policies-childrens-health-compare-countries/
4. Lanzo, Gaetano. "Influenza A vaccination containing adjuvant causes cardiac autonomic dysfunction and inflammation which may transiently increase the risk of cardiovascular events".
http://www.greenmedinfo.com/article/influenza-vaccination-containing-adjuvant-causes-cardiac-autonomic-dysfunction
5. Lindsay, Roseann. "Reclaiming the Vaccine Narrative: "No Such Thing as a 'Safe Vaccine'". http://www.natureofhealing.org/reclaiming-vaccine-narrative-no-thing-safe-vaccine/
6. Mercola, Joseph. "Ask Your Doctor: Are You Being Bribed to Recommend Vaccines?".
http://articles.mercola.com/sites/articles/archive/2012/06/02/bribery-affects-vaccination-rates.aspx
7. Wolfson, Jack, MD. "New FDA-approved Hepatitis B Vaccine Found to Increase Heart Attack Risk by 700%".
http://prepareforchange.net/2017/08/15/new-fda-approved-hepatitis-b-vaccine-found-to-increase-heart-attack-risk-by-700/

Pandemics

Galalae, Kevin. "TURNING NATURE AGAINST MAN: The Role of Pandemics, Vaccines and Genetics in the UN's Plan to Halt Population Growth".
file:///C:/Users/Owner/Downloads/turning-nature-against-man-the-role-of-pandemics-vaccines-and-genetics-in-the-un-s-plan-to-halt-population-growth.pdf

Population Control

1. Editor, Health Freedom Alliance. "Eleven Common Health Symptoms Hint at Global Depopulation 'Slow Kill'".
http://www.healthfreedoms.org/eleven-common-health-symptoms-hint-at-global-depopulation-slow-kill/
2. Galalae, Kevin. Turning Nature against Man: The Role of Pandemics,

Vaccines and Genetics in the UN's Plan to Halt Population Growth".
https://www.researchgate.net/publication/303040648_Turning_Nature_against_Man_The_Role_of_Pandemics_Vaccines_and_Genetics_in_the_UN%27s_Plan_to_Halt_Population_Growth
3. Sarich, Christina. "UN's Role in The UN's Plan to Halt Population Growth by Turning Nature against Us".
http://www.wakingtimes.com/2016/04/14/the-uns-plan-to-halt-population-growth-by-turning-nature-against-us/

Holistic Doctor Deaths
1. Erin, Elizabeth. "Holistic Doctor Death Series: Over 60 Dead in Just over a Year". https://www.healthnutnews.com/recap-on-my-unintended-series-the-holistic-doctor-deaths/
2. Gamble, Foster. "Who is Killing the Healers and Why".
http://www.thrivemovement.com/who-killing-healers-and-why.blog

ETs among Us

Chapter 7

ETs are Already Here

When you consider the story of the Cabal from some distance, it is really an intriguing one – as well as a dark one. But the story gets even more fascinating when ETs enter the picture and you realize the full scope of the secrecy that's taken place around this subject. Indeed, the secret about the ET presence on Earth is perhaps the most compelling one of all.

The fact is ETs have actually been here on our planet for eons of time, with various groups often settling here for thousands of years at a time. As you will see in the following chapters, they are actually our ancestors.

But they're also very much in contact with us in modern times. There have been many thousands of reports about sightings of UFOs since the 1940s, by both civilians and military personnel. And, according to statistics reported by the National UFO Reporting Center outside of Washington DC, since the 1990s, the number of UFO sightings has shot up from 10,000 a year to 45,000 a year.

But it's not just sightings of UFOs that tell us ETs are here with us. There is now a great deal of disclosure about actual contact with ETs here on the ground – as well as out in the solar system away from the earth. Indeed, it's not just metaphysical channels or odd individuals who talk about personal contact with ET races who have landed here (and there are many of these who are very credible). According to a number of insider whistle-blowers, the US government and other world governments have also been in contact with ETs for decades.

Indeed, it's being revealed that until recently there's been a massive cover-up about the many years of contact these governments have had with numerous ET races that have landed here. It will become clear in the next few chapters that what the public has been told about the NASA Space Program and its accomplishments is a phenomenally small piece of the story. Much of what's really been going on has been smothered by cover-up stories.

But, for now, let's review some of the information that has already come out to the public in one way or another, through events the government has not been able to fully suppress.

Roswell Incident

You've likely heard about the Roswell incident over the years – the landing of a crashed UFO in 1947 that NASA immediately moved in to conceal by saying it was simply a crashed weather balloon. Certain people who actually witnessed the craft and saw what happened when the authorities came in have since become adamant whistle-blowers, despite the fact they had been warned and threatened by the authorities to stay quiet about what they had witnessed.

Reports tell us that there were dead bodies of three different races of ETs that had been onboard the craft, and there was also very advanced technology that engineers were subsequently able to reverse-engineer and use since in secret space programs. The government has slowly released some of this advanced technology to the public, but without revealing where it originally came from.

The Phoenix Lights

One of the most spectacular UFO events that's happened in recent history has been called the "Phoenix Lights" which occurred in March of 1997. There was an enormous amount of news coverage of this event, as well as postings on the internet by thousands of people who witnessed it.

As the lighted V-shaped object began moving over Phoenix many people were not just reporting lights hovering in the sky; they were describing the presence of an actual craft of some sort, spanning the size of one or two football fields. The witness reports described many lights on the craft in an organized pattern.

There are some, as shown in the documentary "The Phoenix Lights" who have claimed that the craft was actually one that had been created by the US military through back-engineering crashed ET craft and was not actually an ET craft. And that the display of lights on the craft was to distract the public from some other very intense situation involving the Air Force that was occurring in the mountains close-by. The stories can get so complicated, it is difficult to know what to believe. But the Phoenix Lights event served to wake many up to the reality of space craft in our skies – something that, until very recently, had been officially denied for a long time.

Disclosure

This brings us to the subject of disclosure about ETs as a whole and their presence on and around the earth. There are many involved in the "disclosure community" who are clamoring for full disclosure of everything – which, as we'll see in following chapters, is a great deal more than most people can even imagine. These individuals are concerned about a "partial disclosure" that the Cabal may have in mind – which would slowly reveal only certain aspects of what they, the Cabal, have been up to with their own agenda in keeping so much about their dealings with ETs secret for so long.

Partial disclosure would likely also have a distorted spin on it, as well – one that could make the Cabal appear to be our "saviors" against the "evil aliens". According to some insiders, the Cabal formulated a slow disclosure plan a number of decades ago that would gradually bring about this very scenario.

The plan would include the "revelation" of hostile alien species in our solar system that would eventually bring us to a world war conducted in outer space as well as on the Earth. However, their plan wouldn't actually include any alien species – simply the Cabal using space technology that their secret space programs had been developing and using for a long time.

Mainstream Reports on UFOs

Supporting this idea are reports now in mainstream news that seem to be preparing us for ET life among us. Whether these reports are "planned" as part of the partial disclosure agenda is not clear; some of it may be the result of certain individuals breaking free of the Cabal's hold on them. For instance, as you'll see in following chapters, there are now a number of astronauts who have spoken publicly about the ETs they have seen – or at least have known to exist.

There also have been headlines in 2017 in mainstream news sources. These include "NASA to Disclose Alien Body", "Vault 7 Space Program Secrets" and "Alien life may Already Exist in Our Galaxy". There are science reports on a popular news channel about how our military forces are "preparing for an alien space threat".

In October 2017, the Huffington Post ran an article reporting that three former high-level officials and scientists with "deep black experience" who had operated under "shadows of top-secrecy for decades" had formed an innovative public benefit corporation called "To the Stars Academy of Arts and Science". The institution is designed to advance research into "unexplained phenomena and develop related technology".

Company president and 25-year veteran of the CIA's Directorate of Operations, Tom DeLonge, stated "We believe there are discoveries within our reach that will revolutionize the human experience." Another member of the team and former director of a program in the Department of Defense, Luis Elizondo, confirmed that "UFOs are real and that they have been officially documented". He added: "We are also planning to provide never-before released footage from real US Government systems...not blurry, amateur photos, but real data and real videos."

Another insider in the aerospace industry, Robert Bigelow, has openly come out on the TV program "60 Minutes" saying that he is absolutely convinced that "alien visitors" are here.

And previously, in 2015, a former Canadian defense minister, Paul Hellyer, accused world leaders of concealing the presence of aliens and urged world powers to release what he believed to be hidden data on UFOs. During a keynote speech at the Disclosure Canada Tour at the University of Calgary, he stated:

"Much of the media won't touch [the documents]...You just have to keep working away and hope that someday you get a critical mass. [The public] will say, in one way or another, "Mr. President or Mr. Prime Minister, we want the truth and we want it now because it affects our lives."

Hellyer, 91, first went public with his belief in aliens on Earth in 2005, becoming the first high ranking politician to do so.

And now, just recently, previously-classified information on UFO sightings in the United Kingdom was released.

Majestic-12 Document

One of the most revealing disclosures that has currently occurred, however, is the newly-leaked "Majestic-12" document which describes a variety of extraterrestrial related encounters with humanity. According to the cover page, the document is a preliminary briefing created by the US Defense Intelligence Agency's Office Counter Intelligence on January 8, 1989, addressed to the President.

The document actually refers to four groups of ETs which are listed in order of importance to our planet, and cites whether they are friendly or not: "Earth-like humanoids", "small humanoids or Grays", "non-humanoids EBEs (from worlds in which dominant morphology took a different evolutionary course); and "trans-morphic entities" (those that live in some other dimension or plane than we do).

The Majestic-12 document goes on to describe a "controlled landing" of a flying saucer on March 25, 1948 in Aztec, New Mexico in which there were two dead bodies of small humanoids and one larger adult survivor. This ET reportedly lived under protective custody on the Los Alamos complex for nearly a year and conducted an ongoing diplomatic exchange with the Truman administration.

Secret Space Programs

So all this is now coming out. It's actually a pretty spectacular disclosure that's available for those who are looking for it – especially for the mainstream news to be reporting. However, as we'll see in the following chapters, there is so much more that is yet to be revealed.

As will be clear, at some point it will have to be disclosed that there have been at least two secret space programs in operation for a number of decades, each involved in activities that will be mind-blowing for most people to learn about.

The first covert program exists within the US Air Force and has been operating for many decades. In this program, thanks to reverse-engineering of crashed craft that have landed in various places around the earth, NASA has known how to build and fly its own versions of UFO-type craft and to travel throughout the solar system for a number of decades. As indicated in reports about the Phoenix Lights craft, not all UFOs that have been seen are made or flown by extra-terrestrials – some of them have been made by human beings.

The second program is an even more covert one that has been operated by the US Navy. People in this program, such as Corey Goode, an increasingly vocal whistle-blower, have had extensive dealings and interactions with great numbers of ETs. Apparently, even the US Air Force had not known about this Navy-run program until recently. Insiders refer to the Air Force program as the "MIC" Secret Space Program – as it's run by the military-industrial complex – and the one run by the US Navy simply as the Secret Space Program.

Whistle-Blowers

These two secret space programs have been running for many years. And increasing numbers of people who have been involved in the programs over the years are now uncomfortable with the fact that the people running the programs have not divulged information they've learned about ETs in our solar system – and the presence of much ET activity on and around the earth.

These whistle-blowers are also incensed that the public has not been given the use of ET technology that engineers have managed to reverse-engineer and use for defense purposes, but have not released to the public, despite the fact that it is technology that could impact humanity in very positive ways.

Other groups that whistle-blowers are emerging from are those of high-ranking officials, engineers, astronauts, and others who have been involved as corporate contractors in the space programs. They are also now stepping forward to disclose heretofore top secret information about corporate projects they've worked on under great secrecy over the years.

It's interesting to note that the term "whistle-blower" has generally been used in the past with a somewhat negative connotation, as if the person revealing secret information about the government has threatened "national security" and put the country's safety at risk. With all the information we now have, however, we can move past that old belief and realize that, in actuality, whistle-blowing simply threatens the control mechanisms the global Elite use to enforce their agendas on us.

Disclosure Community

There are a few major players in the disclosure community who speak and write about these secret space programs and from whom I've obtained the information in these next few chapters of this book: David Wilcock, Cobra, Dr. Steven Greer, Corey Goode, Kerry Kassidy, Bill Ryan and Dr. Michael Salla.

Another very important player is James Gilliland, best-seller author, and speaker. With an impressive background in Eastern disciplines, he is best described as a visionary dedicated to the awakening and healing of humanity and the Earth. He has also had ongoing contact with UFOs over the years and has intriguing stories to tell about his experiences. Indeed, he is one of the most clear, heart-centered and tuned-in people I've found in the disclosure community, and I recommend checking out his website and listening to his webcasts.

It's important to note that at this point, not all of the people with information about the ET presence on the Earth agree about the information they are presenting. And, as so often happens in groups dealing with intense and emotional subjects, there are currently strong negative opinions some of these writers and speakers have about each other.

Yet, for the most part, much of their information is the same. As you read the following chapters, decide what feels accurate to you. With an open mind, you may be surprised at how true much of it sounds in the end. If nothing else, you'll likely find it to be a really fascinating story.

If you're interested in learning more about this subject, there are also an increasing number of conferences and gatherings occurring world-wide regarding UFOs and ETs, both online and in person.

ETs are already Here – References

UFO Sightings

1. Dunne, Daisy. "Why have the number of UFO sightings reached an all-time high?" http://www.dailymail.co.uk/sciencetech/article-4253356/UFO-sightings-reached-time-high.html
2. Fox News. "Worldwide UFO sightings hit all-time high." http://video.foxnews.com/v/5339792147001/?#sp=show-clips

Roswell

1. Michael, Tom. "'ROSWELL HAPPENED: Roswell conspiracy theory 'expert' claims UFO crash DID happen... and says a leaked US government document she's seen proves it". https://www.thesun.co.uk/news/3807440/roswell-conspiracy-expert-claims-ufo-crash-did-happen/
2. Wilcock, David. *Ascension Mysteries,* pg.244-48, 251. https://www.amazon.com/Ascension-Mysteries-Revealing-Cosmic-Between-ebook/dp/B0191ZL2EC

Phoenix Lights

1. Kitei, Lynn. "The Phoenix Lights". http://www.thephoenixlights.net/Documentary.htm
2. Walia, Arjun. "Crowd Goes Silent As Actor Kurt Russell Shares His UFO Experience From Phoenix In 1997" http://www.stillnessinthestorm.com/2017/05/crowd-goes-silent-as-actor-kurt-russell-shares-his-ufo-experience-from-phoenix-in-1997.html#more

ETs in the News

1. Anonymous YouTube: "NASA Is About to Announce the Discovery of Intelligent Alien Life" - https://goo.gl/8T62XH
2. Brown, Kaylee. "UK Government To Release All "Secret" British UFO Sighting Files After Election Next Month" http://www.collective-evolution.com/2017/05/25/uk-government-to-release-all-secret-british-ufo-sighting-files-after-election-next-month/
3. Deschamps, Justin. "UFO Disinformation Agent Exposed -- Fake Alien Invasion Scare Sponsored by Air Force Discredits Ufologist | A Case Study http://www.stillnessinthestorm.com/2017/06/ufo-disinformation-agent-exposed-fake-alien-invasion-scare-sponsored-by-air-force-discredits-ufologist-a-case-study.html?utm_source=feedburner&utm_medium=email&utm_campaign=Feed%3A+StillnessInTheStormBlog+%28Stillness+in+the+Storm+Blog%29
4. Disney Studios. "Lost Walt Disney UFO Documentary: Full Uncut". https://www.youtube.com/watch?v=DHunekX1xPw
5. E.T. Disclosure in Media - Compilation of Articles for Week #21. http://www.ascensionwithearth.com/2017/05/et-disclosure-in-media-compilation-of.html

6. Spiegel, Leo. "Aerospace Executive 'Absolutely Convinced' There Are Aliens On Earth".
http://www.huffingtonpost.com/entry/robert-bigelow-ufos-aliens-on-earth_us_592ca03ce4b0065b20b7bfb7
7. Walia, Arjun. "'They're Parked on The Side of the Crater – They're Watching Us!' – When Neil Armstrong Landed On The Moon"
http://www.collective-evolution.com/2017/05/13/theyre-parked-on-the-side-of-the-crater-theyre-watching-us-when-neil-armstrong-landed-on-the-moon/?utm_source=feedburner&utm_medium=email&utm_campaign=Feed%3A+Collective-evolution+%28Collective+Evolution%29
8. Zolfagharif, Ellie. "Governments are HIDING aliens, claims former defence minister: Paul Hellyer urges world leaders to reveal 'secret files'".
http://www.dailymail.co.uk/sciencetech/article-3051151/Governments-HIDING-aliens-claims-former-defence-minister-Paul-Hellyer-urges-world-leaders-reveal-secret-files.html

Majestic-12 Document
Sala, Michael. "New Majestic Document Reveals US Diplomatic Relations with Extraterrestrials". http://exopolitics.org/majestic-document-reveals-us-diplomatic-relations-with-extraterrestrials/

Secret Space Programs and Whistle-Blowers
1. Gilliland, James. http://www.eceti.org/Eceti.IndexII.html
2. Greer, Steven. http://www.disclosureproject.org/
3. Goode, Corey. www.spherebeingalliance.com
4. Salla, Michael. Insiders Reveal Secret Space Programs & Extraterrestrial Alliances. https://www.amazon.com/Insiders-Reveal-Programs-Extraterrestrial-Alliances/dp/0982290284
5. Wilcock, David. https://www.gaia.com/person/david-wilcock

History of Ufology
Deschamps, Justin. "Ufology Researchers Divided but Not Conquered: Exposure of PSYOP to Create Truther "Civil War" -- But it's Not Working"
http://www.stillnessinthestorm.com/2017/08/ufology-researchers-divided-but-not-conquered-exposure-of-psyop-to-create-truther-civil-war-but-it-s-not-working.html?utm_source=feedburner&utm_medium=email&utm_campaign=Feed%3A+StillnessInTheStormBlog+%28Stillness+in+the+Storm%29

Chapter 8

The Disclosure Project

As we've briefly seen, the field of Ufology is one beset by mystery, partial information, misinformation and deliberate disinformation. It's a field in which there has been an inordinate amount of cover-up and in which the truth has been carefully hidden from us.

However, the truth has actually been hidden in plain sight, in that it's obvious something very fishy is going on when we hear that 6.5 trillion dollars have gone "missing" from our defense budget which the Pentagon cannot account for.

Despite the news that has been released to the public of this outrageous amount of missing money, nothing has seemed to happen officially to explain where the money went. So we have to rely on investigators and whistle-blowers to get at least some of the story.

And that story, as was noted in the last chapter, has to do with two secret space programs that have been operating for several decades – one by the US Air Force and the other by the US Navy, neither of which has been officially acknowledged or had oversight by Congress or the president. I will describe first the program operated by the US Air Force.

Father of Disclosure

The information about the secret space program funded by the US Air Force comes mainly from a man who's been called the "Father of Disclosure", Dr. Steven Greer. At one time an "ER doc", Greer eventually became one of the first researchers of Ufology who began serious disclosure on the subject.

He now works full-time as the Director of the Disclosure Project. He is also an author, speaker and director of films about the US UFO cover-up, dedicated to uncovering the unacknowledged information about the presence of ETs in our solar system and on the earth.

Greer appears to be a very down-to-earth kind of guy – a family man with a number of children and grandchildren. He also has a solid esoteric and spiritual background and a primary focus on raising consciousness. He has had numerous personal experiences with ETs. In fact, he has come up with a protocol for calling them in, which he calls "Close Encounters of the Fifth Kind".

For a number of decades now, he has been on a mission to shed light on the fact that we're not alone, that we've never been alone, and that in recent history an ET presence is currently engaging the human race. One thing that sets him aside from many other Ufologists is that he maintains there are only benevolent ETs in contact with us.

He states that these advanced and benevolent ETs from many different civilizations are attempting to steer us in the right direction. He says that they began arriving when we dropped the first nuclear bomb, as this activity created a threat to other planets in the solar system and to the universe as a whole. The ETs also perceived that we were threatening our own race and wished to lend their help.

He maintains that these beings want us to get things under control here before we can be invited into space with them. As much more spiritually-evolved beings and therefore able to easily step in and compel us to do this, they refuse to, believing that we have to learn to control ourselves first. This involves understanding the universal laws of love and harmony, as well as truly understanding who we are and our power to affect many others in the universe.

Center for Study of ET Intelligence and Disclosure Project

In the early days of his interest in UFOs, Greer simply wanted to make contact with ETs. And he was very successful with this, even when he was with groups of people he invited to participate in these encounters.

What surprised him after one of his most successful contacts, however, was that he was subsequently contacted by military intelligence people. Some of them asked him hostile questions which came down to: "Who do you think you are?!" Others were more friendly, as they had had their own experiences with UFOs and ETs. Due to his encounters with these intelligence agents, he began realizing the nature of the government secrecy and cover-up of UFO knowledge.

As his curiosity and irritation at the secrecy grew, in 1990 he decided to create a center to conduct research into the whole ET phenomenon, the Center for the Study of Extraterrestrial Intelligence (CSETI). And then he added the Disclosure Project, created specifically to seek the disclosure of UFO information that was being suppressed by the government.

Since then, through this program, he has been able to organize and gather over 800 whistle-blowers who have given very credible witness testimony through signed statements, documents and filmed interviews about the cover-up of information regarding ET contact on earth.

Indeed, through the years, Greer has amassed a great deal of credibility. He and his team have interviewed astronauts, colonels, generals, high level defense contractors, and government officials who have testified to their personal, first-hand experience regarding ET/UFO secrecy and new energy technology suppression.

As it turns out, the part of the Cabal running this covert program is comprised of those from three different sources: those in the military, the corporate world, and the intelligence community. Their projects are unacknowledged, so there's no oversight over them.

Evidently, as we've seen in the chapter on Mind Control, people from the intelligence community have traditionally given huge cash bribes to the mainstream media to kill stories about any of this secrecy. The MSM will simply not cover any of the story. When snippets of the truth do enter into a story, journalists have generally attempted to discredit it.

Astronaut Whistle-Blowers

Among the many insiders who have given testimony to their experiences with UFOs and ETs, are an increasing number of astronauts who were on the Apollo & Gemini missions. Edgar Mitchell, in particular, has reported that he saw UFOs following his ship to the moon and that he also saw ET structures there. Other high-level officers have testified that they have lived and worked on bases, both on the moon and Mars.

Many of them attest to the fact that ETs have been visiting us for a long time. Others, especially those who worked in the corporations employed by the government to test and reverse-engineer ET technology found on crashed craft, are also speaking out. Ben Rich, former director of Lockheed Skunkworks from 1975-1991, reported that he had worked on teams to create technology way beyond what was generally known by the public – or government officials, for that matter:

> "We already have the means to travel among the stars, but these technologies are locked up in black projects, and it would take an act of God to ever get them out to benefit humanity. Anything you can imagine, we already know how to do it...We now have technology to take ET home. No, it won't take someone's lifetime to do it...We now have the capability to travel to the stars."

Indeed, as Greer points out, the term "UFO" is actually a misnomer. These flying objects are very well known and identified by the military. Even before Roswell, engineers had been studying ET technology; already in 1954, the US had discovered how ET craft worked.

It probably isn't surprising that whistle-blowers, especially in the early days, have been known to be assassinated. Three different people on Greer's team alone were murdered during the 1990s. Horrified by these deaths, Greer decided to completely quit his research and disclosure efforts. But he was finally convinced to resume his work by people on the inside of the projects who pledged to give him protection.

It seems to be apparent today that more and more intelligence and military people want disclosure now – particularly about the existence of free energy devices and the means to eradicate poverty on the planet. But still, after all this time, the Elite remains in control of keeping all the covert information under wraps – except for those savvy enough to find it on the internet and certain television programs.

Passion for Disclosure

Greer has given out a massive amount of information over the years through a number of speeches, articles and books. He has also produced two films on the subject: "Sirius" and "Unacknowledged". His eloquence and passion for disclosure are compelling.

In one of his articles, he stated:

> "The UFO matter is not so much a mystery as a matter deliberately obfuscated and mystified. Confusion and a lack of clarity serve the larger covert goal of keeping it off the long-range radar of society while power and plans are consolidated quietly. And the one thing more dangerous to society than all this secrecy is a planned, contrived disclosure run by the keepers of the secrets...
>
> It will be a false disclosure – one born out of the age-old bane of human existence: selfishness and greed. Greed for power. Greed for control. Greed for domination."

He proclaims that these clandestine projects are illegal, shadowy operations and are a direct threat to national and world security concerns. Their "black funding" status deprives genuine security, intelligence and military programs of much needed support and technological resources.

He further elaborates:

> "Such 'shadowy' projects hide within the vast bureaucracy of government, military intelligence, corporate, laboratory and institute operations in the U.S. and abroad - compartmented away from the public, the Congress and usually even the President, CIA Director and Secretary of Defense. The illegal nature of such projects, their highly compartmented nature and their large financial resources prevents normal oversight and control by the government of the people."

Decoy, Distract and Trash

Greer also bemoans the fact that certain individuals who have had close interactions (a.k.a. "abductees" and "contactees") with UFOs and their ET occupants are being forced to deny any positive or edifying aspects of their encounters, and are left to dwell only on the frightening and negative aspects of the experience.

Indeed, whistle-blowing is no easy task – nor is it a safe one. Many speak about the fact that certain people who have disclosed secrets have ended up being ostracized, losing their jobs, and sometimes even losing their lives. Greer said he's been told that informants have been traditionally subjected to what's known as the "DDT campaign" – Decoy, Distract & Trash.

When a whistle-blower first comes on the scene with information, the first thing that happens is that paid government employees create fake data known as "disinformation". This they release into the same media source that featured the informant's information (this is the "decoy"). The disinformation then distracts people and eventually encourages them to dismiss the whistle-blower as a fraud (which is, of course, the "trashing").

However, even despite this, whistle-blowers do continue to come forward. And, as we'll see in the following chapters, their testimony is riveting.

Fudged Moon Landings

One of the interesting revelations through insider testimony is that much of what supposedly happened on the US missions to the moon is being questioned. A while back in early 2017, the Russian government called for an international investigation into the U.S. moon landings due to missing samples and photos not released to the public. This created a new interest about what really happened when the US went into space and led some to question if they even went there at all.

But then it got even more interesting as a number of sources, including multiple Apollo astronauts, academicians, and high ranking military informants began reporting what they'd actually experienced or witnessed on these missions – versus what had officially been reported. According to Bob Dean, a United States Army Command Sergeant Major who served as an intelligence analyst, more footage of the moon exploration exists, erased and hidden, which we have never been told about.

Another source stated that forty rolls of film of the Apollo Program were erased from the flight to the moon, around the moon, and landings on the moon. Astronaut Neil Armstrong revealed that the photos shown to the public of the moon landings had originally had towers, buildings, ruins, and active bases airbrushed out of them.

Also, according to multiple sources, after landing, the Apollo astronauts transmitted that they were being watched by very large extraterrestrial vehicles. Indeed, there's evidence that while Armstrong and Aldrin were on the lunar surface, Neil switched to the medical channel, and spoke directly with the chief medical officer saying, "They're here, they're parked on the side of the crater. They're watching us." And another reported: "There are other ships here – they are enormous."

Armstrong told Greer he wished he could talk about it – but that he'd been warned that if he spoke about what *really* happened during the moon landing, that he, his wife, and children would all be killed. It was put to him this bluntly.

Secret ET Technology

The Disclosure Project team has hundreds of witnesses whose testimony, government documents and related evidence prove not only that UFOs exist – but that some of them are made by humans using "extraordinary breakthroughs" in physics, energy generation and propulsion, due to the back-engineering efforts of scientific teams.

In short, the technologies needed to replace the internal combustion engine and fossil fuels already exist in these clandestine projects – projects that the American public has paid for.

Indeed, we already have available solutions to all global environmental crises we are faced with, as well as solutions to end poverty across the earth. With the ET technology that engineers and physicists have figured out, there would be no need for coal, gas, petroleum, or oil. It would mean goodbye to fossil fuels. All the corporation and Cabal interests in these fuels would become worthless. Greer states that the Cabal has plans to hold onto the scientific information so they can eventually use it for their own benefit – essentially to scare people about "aliens", thereby weakening them.

Aside from technology that could assist people across the world in some essential ways, there is also technology that could be very useful for our lives. Take healing technology built into a bed, for instance, that helps you heal, as was depicted in the movie "Elysium". Or technology that takes you to another continent or planet in an instant, using teleportation – or allows you to experience your wildest fantasy in a holodeck, like in Star Trek. Imagine simply thinking something and your computer does it. All this kind of fantasy technology already exists here on earth. We just don't have access to it.

Perhaps the most confusing thing the Cabal forces within the space program have done is to create flying saucers and other craft, mimicking the ET technology that was found on crashed ET crafts – and then having these crafts show up in the skies as if they're controlled by ETs.

Aside from causing confusion, this practice has also caused some real damage when one of the human-made vessels has crashed and harmed or killed people. Not knowing that humans know how to create these kinds of craft, people of course jump to the conclusion that there must be ETs who crashed. True to form, the government never sets us straight. They can thus avoid blame for the damage done.

President and CIA Director Excluded from the Secrets

In Chapter 4, we saw that the US president is often not apprised of many of the secrets the Cabal hold. Here too we see this, in that secrets about the ET presence on earth are usually kept from the president, and at times from the CIA Director in an administration. If people in these offices are not part of the Cabal and would not go along with their agenda, they simply are not told about the projects.

Greer discovered this through the dozens and dozens of testimonies he heard from the military that attest to it. He also learned how low on the secrecy scale presidents and CIA directors are, through the reports of staff members of ex-presidents and CIA directors – and even living ex-presidents and CIA directors, themselves. These people have reached out to him, wanting the information he has, as they had been denied it when serving in their political offices.

One who had been on Eisenhower's staff described the president's ire in knowing secrets were being kept from him. WikiLeaks recently revealed letters from JFK held by the CIA, in which he was asking the CIA for information they had about UFOs; he evidently knew he was being denied the information. Reagan apparently also found out about ETs and was going to tell the public about it. That was when an assassination attempt was made on him.

And Jimmy Carter was another one who became very angry when he found out that Greer had learned information from insiders that Carter had never been privy to as president. He himself had evidently seen a UFO when he was governor; and when he mentioned it to Washington officials, he was threatened to keep his mouth shut.

Progress of the Disclosure Project

Over the past 30 years, Greer and his team have met with senior CIA, Pentagon, White House and other political figures, advocating a general disclosure on UFOs, extraterrestrial intelligence and related energy and propulsion systems currently held by illegal "classified" projects. There were a number of times when former Apollo astronaut Edgar Mitchell joined Greer in meetings within the Pentagon about this issue. And yet, none of the meetings has created an official agenda for disclosure.

Even when Greer has gone straight to the Press, there have been no visible results. As far back as May of 2001, over twenty military, intelligence, government, corporate and scientific witnesses came forward with him at the National Press Club in Washington, DC to establish the reality of UFOs, extraterrestrial life forms, and resulting advanced energy and propulsion technologies.

Greer has presented at other press conferences since, revealing even more information, most recently in 2015. The weight of this first-hand testimony, along with supporting government documentation and other evidence, should have established without any doubt the reality of these phenomena. And yet, to date, it has not.

Partial or Skewed Disclosure

One thing Greer is concerned about is a disclosure about UFOs and ETs made by the Powers that Be that will only be partial – and that it will be tweaked in such a way as to misinform and further confuse and frighten people.

In his book *Extraterrestrial Contact: The Evidence and Implications,* he describes the kind of disclosure he believes the world needs: "An honest one, an open one. One which replaces secrecy with democracy. A disclosure which is peaceful, scientific and hopeful."

In this ideal scenario for disclosure, excessive secrecy which lacks executive branch and congressional oversight would be ended. Humanity would begin to entertain open contact with other civilizations, with peaceful engagement as the goal.

Furthermore, technologies which are currently suppressed would be allowed to be disseminated: Pollution would end. An economy of abundance and social justice would be firmly established. And global environmental destruction and world poverty would become a faint memory.

But he's naturally aware that there are hugely powerful interests who dread this scenario. For them, it would be the end of the world as they know it. The end of centralized, elite power. The end of a controlled geopolitical order which today leaves "nearly 90% of the people of the Earth barely out of the Stone Age".

As a result, finally despairing of ever motivating officials to disclose about the ET presence on earth, Greer in recent years has finally turned to the public with an impassioned appeal to create a "groundswell" of support of full disclosure to help cause it to occur.

Attempts to Discredit Greer

There have been, of course, numerous efforts in a variety of ways to suppress Greer's attempt to bring a close to the secrecy behind the Air Force's Secret Space Program. And other attempts to keep him from getting public support behind him that he believes would compel the disclosure to happen.

However, there are others in the Disclosure Community itself who are also saying things to discredit him. Some, as we'll see in the following chapters, staunchly assert that not all ETs on and around our planet are benevolent, believing it's actually dangerous to declare there are only benevolent ETs.

Whatever the truth, it's important to remember that even if Greer isn't totally accurate or on target with all he's proclaiming, he has probably done more over a greater amount of time in bringing awareness to the public about the clandestine space projects than anyone else out there.

Disclosure Project - References

Steven Greer

1. Greer, Steven. http://www.disclosureproject.org/
2. Greer, Steven. *Extraterrestrial Contact: The Evidence and Implications.*
3. Greer, Steven. "When Disclosure Serves Secrecy".
http://siriusdisclosure.com/cseti-papers/when-disclosure-serves-secrecy/
4. Greer, Steven. "Disclosure and 9/11".
file:///C:/Users/Owner/Documents/work/collective%20consc%20book/CC%20%20Disclosure%20Project%20Greer/disclosure%20project%20articles/disclosure911.pdf
5. Greer, Steven. "Unacknowledged".
http://siriusdisclosure.com/unacknowledged-film/
6. Greer, Steven. "Sirius". https://www.youtube.com/watch?v=5C_-HLD21hA
Center for Study of Extraterrestrial Intelligence (CSETI)
www.new.cseti.org/

Astronaut Whistle-Blowers

1. Spiegel, Lee. "Leaked Emails Reveal Former Astronaut Wanted To Meet With Obama Official About Alien Life".
http://www.huffingtonpost.com/entry/wikileaks-emails-aliens_us_57fd14b4e4b068ecb5e1eb1f
2. Walia, Arjun. "They're Parked on The Side of the Crater – They're Watching Us!" – When Neil Armstrong Landed On The Moon".
http://www.collective-evolution.com/2017/05/13/theyre-parked-on-the-side-of-the-crater-theyre-watching-us-when-neil-armstrong-landed-on-the-moon/

Disclosure

1. Frye, Megan. "Aliens: Earth's Future is Not Written in Stone".
http://www.rumormillnews.com/cgi-bin/forum.cgi?read=76079
2. James, Preston. The Coming Shift to Cosmic Fascism (Part III)
http://www.veteranstoday.com/2017/05/24/the-coming-shift-to-cosmic-fascism-part-iii/
3. Rojas, Alexander. "Has UFO Disclosure Already Happened?".
http://www.huffingtonpost.com/alejandro-rojas/has-ufo-disclosure-alread_b_3156705.html
4. Walia, Arjun. "JFK's Pilot Reveals What The President Knew About UFOs & Extraterrestrials". http://www.collective-evolution.com/2017/05/31/jfks-ex-pilot-reveals-what-the-president-knew-about-ufos-extraterrestrials/

Fudged Moon Landings

1. "Dr. Greer: 1969 Moon landing WAS faked"
https://ocseti.wordpress.com/2016/08/01/dr-greer-1969-moon-landing-was-faked/
2. Icke, David. "Dr. Steven Greer on David Icke, The Moon Landing, Giant UFOs". https://www.youtube.com/watch?v=k0MyZqdHqiI
3. *Walia, Arjun.* "They're Parked on The Side of the Crater – They're Watching Us!" – When Neil Armstrong Landed On The Moon".
http://www.collective-evolution.com/2017/05/13/theyre-parked-on-the-side-of-the-crater-theyre-watching-us-when-neil-armstrong-landed-on-the-moon/

Secret ET Technology

Marcotte, Amanda. "WATCH: Is the government hiding secret technology".
http://www.salon.com/2017/05/29/watch-is-the-government-hiding-secret-technology-brought-to-earth-by-aliens/
Presidents and UFO Info
Greer, Steven. *Unacknowledged: An Expose of the World's Greatest Secret.*
https://www.amazon.com/Unacknowledged-Expose-Worlds-Greatest-Secret/dp/1943957045

Chapter 9

Further Secrets about ETs, the Moon and Mars

According to certain UFO/ET investigators, there is much more to be disclosed about secret space programs than what Greer has disclosed. There are three main sources I use for this information presented in the next few chapters: David Wilcock, Corey Goode, and a man with the code name of "Cobra".

David Wilcock, author, speaker, and avid researcher of UFO/ET phenomena is an investigator who, like Greer, offers impeccable documentation for everything he discloses. Many of his whistle-blowers have been part of covert space projects operated by members in the US Navy – as opposed to those Greer has apparently worked with, who have been involved with projects run by the US Air Force. It became clear recently through Wilcock's insiders that many top officials in the Air Force projects were unaware that the Navy also had a program of their own which was involved in even deeper secrecy.

Corey Goode, a quiet and somewhat shy man, has an intriguing story of spending twenty years on the dark side of the moon and other places in the solar system. Identified as an intuitive empath at the age of six, he was recruited by the secret space program run by the US Navy. He trained and served in the program from 1976-1987. Toward the end of his time there, he was assigned to fill a support role for a rotating Earth Delegate Seat in an ET Federation Council and played an important role in communicating with non-terrestrial beings. He now serves as a very vocal whistle-blower.

Cobra is known as a "Pleiadian contactee" who has been working for over 35 years with the Light Forces that are part of what's known as the "Resistance Movement" operated by ET beings involved in resisting the Dark Forces, comprised of both ET and human forces. His codename "Cobra" stems from the term "Compression Breakthrough" – otherwise known as "the Event" – a phenomenon that will be described in full in Chapter 16. He has been told to remain anonymous by The Resistance while continuing to strive to prepare humanity for the coming global events.

Galactic Battle

One important difference between the information these three present and that of Greer's is that they not only give evidence that there are definitely ETs in our skies and on the earth among us – but that they are also living inside the earth. And further, very importantly, they assert that many of these ETs with us and around us are not at all benevolent. Indeed, according to their evidence, there are some powerful groups that are extremely malevolent toward humanity – and they have essentially been holding humanity hostage for many thousands of years.

In addition, according to this evidence, the Cabal, as we know them today, are apparently descendants of those who were the off-spring created by the breeding of these ETs with humans long, long ago – and the ETs still existing on Earth, until very recently, have been using the Cabal to help them keep control over humanity.

The main focus of these whistle-blowers, however, is on the battle they deem to be a very ancient one between dark and light ET forces. And how, for the first time, the benevolent ETs are finally winning – with the help of what is called the "Earth Alliance" and the "Inner Earth Alliance", all which will be described in more detail in Chapter 13.

Before the "Science Fiction!" bell goes off in your mind, I invite you, as always, to keep an open mind about all of this. As I've suggested, when you read or hear the evidence backing up these kinds of claims, you may experience a surprising knowing in your gut that there is at least some truth to all of it – if not a lot.

ETs Working at NASA

Wilcock has intriguing testimony from a number of whistle-blowers from within the military and intelligence communities who speak about ETs working with NASA engineers. One of his main insiders, William Tompkins, an aerospace engineer recently deceased, gave Wilcock an immense amount of information over the years about the many covert projects the Secret Space Program has created.

One of the interesting aspects of Tomkins' career was when he actually worked side by side with certain "human-like" ETs who blended in with the NASA crew. He claims they helped his team design the rockets and systems that became the Apollo program.

ET Bases on the Moon

As in the recent revelations by astronauts that Greer has interviewed, there is also testimony Wilcock has from a number of insiders that there are many ancient ruins on the moon left by ETs, some which existed even before civilization is known to have occurred on earth. Many of them are obelisks similar to the Egyptian ones found on the earth and are aligned in much the same way.

Also, numerous ET civilizations are currently operating on the dark side of the moon that cannot be seen from the earth. There are buildings that are miles high; some are actually floating, and many are in geometric configurations. But since the moon has no atmosphere, numerous bases have been built below the surface. In some places, structures are 20 to 50 miles deep. They're divided into many different levels, full of buildings, rooms, and military equipment.

What's fascinating is that there are numerous different races of ETs who have created bases there, many of whom have been historically in conflict with each other. But they all seem to tolerate each other's presence, as if in tacit agreement that the moon doesn't belong to any one group. It's "neutral" territory.

Another curious aspect of the intel given about the moon that may be distressing to those with romantic notions is that it is not the natural celestial body we all assume it to be: it is actually something that was *built* eons ago to serve as a vehicle that could be driven from one star system to another.

At times it was evidently also used to carry animals and plants from one planet to another. At some point during a period of fierce battling between ET races, the moon was damaged to such an extent that it could no longer be used for this purpose. But it's now referred to by those in the know as the "ark".

US Bases on the Moon

Perhaps some of the most interesting intel about US bases on the moon is given by Corey Goode, who reveals how while in the program on the moon he was inducted into as a child, he met and worked with numerous ETs of many different races. He describes a number of these races and how they at times attempt to work together.

He relates that once his 20-year contract was up, his superiors in the program employed a commonly-used practice of erasing all his memories of his time spent in the program. This erasure apparently worked for a while; but then at some point memories started filtering through, causing him great anguish. And this is when he realized he needed to begin revealing details of the program he'd been in and all the harm the secrecy was doing to people on Earth. His passion in speaking as a whistle-blower, although quiet and contained, is vividly palpable.

Through these speaking engagements and interviews, Goode describes how he is continuing his work on his own at this point through remaining in direct physical contact with a group of ETs who have contacted him. He calls them the "Blue Avians" (of the Sphere Being Alliance). These beings have requested that he serve as a delegate to interface with multiple ET Federations and Councils, liaise with the Secret Space Alliance Council, and deliver important messages to humanity.

In his presentations, Goode reveals what he says is the true story of humanity's celestial presence. He also gives an extraterrestrial message which conveys details of the coming collective ascension for humankind. He states that the Sphere Being Alliance is here to guide us through the ascension process – but that it is up to us to enact the changes that will lead to full disclosure and ascension.

Unsurprisingly, not everyone is happy about Goode's remarkable rise and the widespread public attention he has gathered with his ground-breaking testimony. His life has been threatened a number of times. And, as with Greer, UFO researchers have also attempted to discredit him. It's true that Goode has no hard scientific evidence to back up his claims. However, his claims have been corroborated by a number of other insiders who've reported to Wilcock.

Also another whistle-blower has come forward describing a similar program she was inducted into in much the same way Goode had been: Sierra Neblina. She describes similar experiences, including receiving serious threats of harm to her family if she continued the work she began after recovering her memories in the program to investigate military cover-up of ET contact and human abductions.

German Bases on the Moon and Mars

According to the intel of a number of secret space program insiders, the Germans were actually the first human group to make it to the moon and set up a base there in the 1930s. They also evidently made it to Mars and set up a base there.

This was discovered by Americans who spoke with captured German scientists and spies during World War II. One of these insiders mentioned earlier, William Tompkins, revealed to Wilcock a great deal about the intel given to him by these men. Known as the "Grandfather of Disclosure", Tomkins worked in Naval Intelligence debriefing spies who had worked in German aerospace companies. Tomkins also stated that the Germans were the first in the world to discover the ruins of an ancient ET race in Antarctica and also on Mars.

US Bases on Mars

Other fascinating testimony about Mars bases came from another of Wilcock's insiders who revealed that he had worked for a number of years on Mars repairing different types of advanced equipment that were important for the survival of the human race. He stated that in this work, he worked side by side with a number of different species of ETs. He described how his communication with them was mind-to-mind, and how he always experienced a sense of extreme spiritual bliss when this communication would occur.

Other insiders have reported that our bases on Mars are massive – and that they are located in a lava tube into which an oxygen blend is pumped so that humans can breathe. There are also reports that since the 1950s, people have been taken to Mars to both live and work with ETs.

In fact, there are those who claim that the Mars projects not only exist – but that they actually include a type of "slave colony" into which people over the years have been abducted. One of these whistle-blowers is Laura Magdalene Eisenhower, the great-granddaughter of the former president. She states that she was recruited to join a Mars colony supposedly for the "continuity of the human race". She says she refused, knowing the true nature of these colonies.

Several other secret space program insiders, such as Randy Cramer and Corey Goode, also assert that for decades various secret government programs have abducted millions of people and moved them to Mars. These numbers sound staggering; but again, much of this information has been given by people with documentation showing they actually worked in these space projects. Recruits are told they will live in "technological opulence", only to discover upon their arrival that the colony is managed as a "slave plantation".

Just recently, a very vocal whistle-blower on the scene, Robert David Steele, has spoken up about the "Mars Slave Colony" the US has been running on Mars for years. Steele is a former CIA clandestine services case officer. It's important to note that although the MSM attempted to brush his evidence off as conspiracy theory, NASA actually found it necessary to deny the reality of such a colony – something the agency had apparently never been compelled to do previously with "conspiracy theories."

ET Technology

As we've seen in the testimony given to Greer and others, reports from Wilcock, Goode and Cobra also confirm that there is ET technology the US has had for decades that the public knows nothing about.

Military defense contractors have been manufacturing a great variety of products that would absolutely transform life on earth if they were to be released. Among others, author Col. Philip Corso, in his book *The Day After Roswell*, describes boxes of "foreign technology" that have been given to different defense contractors over the years with instructions that their engineers reverse-engineer it.

The advanced technology recovered from crashed ET craft included that which could create space ships much more advanced than that produced by humans. It also included cloaking technology which has been used by the military to cloak naval vessels, aircraft and spacecraft. In fact, according to some sources, our skies are filled with masked craft.

Wilcock further describes other reverse-engineered technology consisting of technology to help teleport people out into space or assist them to time travel. Devices providing anti-gravity and free energy have also been around for a very long time, as well as very advanced health technology that could assist humanity in ways that are inconceivable to us at this point.

Human scientists in these secret programs are also now able to create "portals" into different dimensions, places, and times. There are insider stories that describe early trials of this particular technology in which the human subjects in the experiments were actually lost and never found. In later trials, the scientists eventually learned how to get people back; but it's a bit frightening to hear of these earlier experiments and what happens behind the scenes as human scientists play with advanced technology they don't yet understand.

Another fascinating type of technology that has been reverse-engineered from a crashed UFO has been called the "Montauk Chair", named after the city in New York in which it was created. This chair is designed to attune to the mind of anyone who sits in it – and to produce in physical form in the room whatever the person is thinking about.

Stargate Network

An intriguing discovery that occurred through the experiments with the Montauk Chair is something they've called the "Stargate Network". Again, this sounds eerily like science fiction – or something that "woo woo" channels or psychics speak about. But the network evidently actually exists and is accessible from our current reality.

Scientists estimate that this network was originally designed about 10,000 years ago by a highly advanced ET race called the "Elders". It was designed to allow for peaceful exploration and communication with a variety of worlds, even outside our galaxy. It allows travel from place to place through a "cosmic web". Each planet with intelligent life has been given its own Stargate.

It is currently still used by certain benevolent ETs in coming to Earth. However, they have the understanding that they need to follow a "prime directive" built into the network, which is to conceal themselves at this point so as not to frighten human beings. It's been found that taking a trip through the Stargate Network involves a "wormhole ride", and that for most of the human beings taking the ride, it is extremely traumatic. Subjects who have been traumatized by this experience have come to be known as people having "transdimensional disorder."

The Cabal's Plan for ET Technology

Again, all this may sound like science fiction – information and ideas that people have picked up from all the books and movies out there featuring similar things. But as described in an earlier chapter, that's exactly what the Cabal wants us to think.

It's why they have been purposely leaking ideas about these technologies to authors, screen writers and video game producers for years. They've wanted to get the ideas into these forms of entertainment so that if anyone participating in the secret programs decides to leak information about what is happening in them, it's ensured they will be dismissed for making up a story up based on a movie, book or game available to the public.

The Cabal apparently has designs for their own disclosure about these technologies at some point with a plan to "dazzle" the public. They might, for instance, suddenly present to the world their knowledge of clean, limitless energy, as if it were a brand new invention we could be grateful to them for – when all along, it's been known for almost a hundred years.

Partial Disclosure

Like Greer, Wilcock and others are concerned about the partial disclosure that seems to be currently happening. Whether this disclosure is what the Cabal always planned to be doing at this time, or whether they have had to start it due to pressure from the unwanted disclosure that is already happening, is unknown.

But if you'll notice, headlines even in the mainstream news are appearing, saying things like: "Alien life may already exist in our galaxy". Or you can read that there has been a release of certain formerly classified documents from the CIA Vault 7, in which it is stated that we have already had some contact with ETs.

It appears that the Cabal is giving up tidbits of information – but these tidbits have a negative and frightening spin on them so that they can stay in control of the real information. And, very importantly, it's clear to some that this spin in the gradual disclosure is leading up to a plan in which the Cabal hopes to convince humanity that we may be attacked by hostile aliens someday soon. This way, everyone can be prepared for the next huge planetary war the Cabal, themselves, will create. For example, the NY Times recently featured a long article entitled "Greetings ET (Please Don't Murder Us)".

The Cabal is Losing

Despite these well-laid plans of the Cabal, however, the good news is they are now being beaten in their own game. There are currently too many credible whistle-blowers out there telling the true story. Also, as we'll see in Chapter 13, an alliance has formed of many in the Pentagon and intelligence agencies – as well as in the secret space programs themselves – who want the secrecy to end. Much is afoot at this point to bring these operations out in the open and to end all the corruption and control games.

And, very importantly, these whistle-blowers and other "White Hats" are eager to release the much-advanced ET technology that will benefit all of humanity, such as anti-aging and free-energy technology. What most informants want is full disclosure of all that has been held secret – not partial or skewed disclosure – and for this disclosure to happen now.

And, with any luck, it just may.

More Secrets about ETs, the Moon and Mars - References

David Wilcock
1. Wilcock, David. *Ascension Mysteries: Revealing the Cosmic Battle between Good and Evil.* https://www.amazon.com/Ascension-Mysteries-Revealing-Cosmic-Between-ebook/dp/B0191ZL2EC
2. Wilcock, David. https://www.gaia.com/person/david-wilcock
3. Wilcock, David. "Ascension Mysteries: Cosmic Battle between Good and Evil". https://www.youtube.com/watch?v=7-ZWzwNMsxQ

Corey Goode
Goode, Corey. www.spherebeingalliance.com

Sierra Neblina
Neblina, Sierra. http://www.galacticu.com/about.html

Galactic Battle
1. Goode, Corey. "Cosmic Disclosure: the Dark Fleet." https://spherebeingalliance.com/blog/transcript-cosmic-disclosure-the-dark-fleet.html
2. Wilcock, David. "Full Disclosure and Ascension: The War Has Gone Hot!" http://divinecosmos.com/start-here/davids-blog/1201-full-disclosure-asc-ii?showall=1&limitstart=
3. Wilcock, David. *Ascension Mysteries,* pg. 435. https://www.amazon.com/Ascension-Mysteries-Revealing-Cosmic-Between-ebook/dp/B0191ZL2EC

ET Bases on the Moon
Wilcock, David. *Ascension Mysteries,* pg. 252-56, 275-304, 387, 389 ("ark") https://www.amazon.com/Ascension-Mysteries-Revealing-Cosmic-Between-ebook/dp/B0191ZL2EC
US Bases on the Moon
Wilcock, David. *Ascension Mysteries,* pg. 256, 249
German Bases on Moon and Mars
1. Salla, Michael. "German Secret Societies Colonized Mars in the 1930s". http://exopolitics.org/german-secret-societies-colonized-mars-in-1940s/
2. Terziski, Vladimir. "Half a Century of the German Moon Base". https://www.bibliotecapleyades.net/luna/esp_luna_46.htm

US & ET Bases on Mars
1. Editor, Stillness in the Storm. "NASA Denies Mars Slave Colony Exists, Despite Claims of Ex-CIA Agent and Whistleblowers". http://www.stillnessinthestorm.com/2017/07/nasa-denies-mars-slave-colony-exists-despite-claims-of-ex-cia-agent-and-whistleblowers.html?utm_source=feedburner&utm_medium=email&utm_campaign=Feed%3A+StillnessInTheStormBlog+%28Stillness+in+the+Storm%29

2. Wilcock, David. *Ascension Mysteries,* pg. 313, 412.
https://www.amazon.com/Ascension-Mysteries-Revealing-Cosmic-Between-ebook/dp/B0191ZL2EC

ET Technology
1. Corso, Philip. *The Day After Roswell.*
2. Futurism: "Fusion Breakthrough Puts Us One Step Closer to Limitless Clean Energy" - https://goo.gl/MG8HGB

Stargate Network
1. Wilcock, David. *Ascension Mysteries,* pg. 331.
https://www.amazon.com/Ascension-Mysteries-Revealing-Cosmic-Between-ebook/dp/B0191ZL2EC

ETs in Mainstream Media
1. Johnson, Steve. "Greetings, E.T. (Please Don't Murder Us.)"
https://www.nytimes.com/2017/06/28/magazine/greetings-et-please-dont-murder-us.html?emc=eta1

Chapter 10

ETs inside the Earth

At this point, you've probably accepted the fact that ETs are here among us today, both in our skies and, to some degree, on the Earth with us. So perhaps it won't be too much of a surprise to learn that that there have also been ETs who have been living *inside* the earth for millions of years, as well—and and they still reside there today.

This information from many different sources tells us both that the earth is actually hollow and that ETs have been living there. Ancient texts, modern day metaphysical sources, and space program insiders all describe this reality.

The Agarthans

There is much that has been written about a civilization of ETs who have lived within the Earth for millennia, known as the "Agarthans". Author and spiritual researcher Joshua David Stone has written extensively about this civilization.

He points out that Buddhist texts actually refer to Agartha's existence. They describe its inhabitants as a race of advanced men and women who occasionally come to the surface to oversee the development of the human race. The texts also state that millions of inhabitants live there in many cities, and that their capital is Shamballah.

These texts claim that the master of this Inner Earth world has given instructions over time to the Dalai Lamas of Tibet, who have been his terrestrial representatives. Until the current Dali Lama was forced to leave Tibet, the messages were said to be transmitted through secret tunnels connecting this inner world with Tibet.

This is especially interesting in that Hindu texts also allude to an ancient place called Agartha within the Earth. The *Bhagavad Gita* tells the story of an "emissary from Agartha" who arrived in an air vehicle. As we'll see in Chapter 13, Insider Cobra speaks at length about the "Agarthan Network", an alliance of the Agarthan ETs who have joined with Galactic Forces to fight the Dark Forces.

Metaphysical Sources about Inner Earth Civilizations

In addition, there are a number of other sources over the years also referring to civilizations existing inside the Earth. Sheldan Nidle tells us that the outer and inner crusts of the Earth have very similar topography: Both comprise oceans, continents, mountain ranges, lakes, and rivers. What's different is that the inner crust faces the Earth's core rather than the sky.

He says that this core glows and is surrounded by a cloudy veil. The light given off in the "cavern worlds" is more diffuse than the light of the Sun, so the daylight there is softer and gentler than on the Earth's external surface. Nidle claims that this land is the last living remnant of a colony known to many as "Lemuria". This ancient civilization, in its original form, was a surface society with a subterranean component.

According to Nidle, the primary capital city of Lemuria was situated on a large island that sank beneath the Pacific about 25,000 years ago. But a secondary capital city, Shamballah, survived in a cavern far beneath the city of Lhasa in modern Tibet. Like the ancient texts, Nidle too asserts that many tunnels connect Shamballah to the surface in the Himalayas.

A number of other authors and channels speak about an Inner Earth civilization known as "Telos", which they say is located beneath Mt. Shasta in northern California. Two of these channels, Dianne Robbins and Aurelia Louise Jones, tell us this civilization came from Lemuria before a thermal nuclear war took place – a war that might have caused the "great flood" ancient texts speak of.

Evidence Based on Reports of Arctic Explorers

But the descriptions of an inner Earth world are not limited to ancient texts and metaphysical writings. There are people around the world who have investigated, and claim to have even visited, these inner Earth civilizations.

One of the first to write about the Earth being hollow with openings at its poles was an American explorer, William Reed, author of *Phantom of the Poles,* published in 1906. Reed estimated that the crust of the Earth has a thickness of 800 miles, with a hollow interior of 6,400 miles. He summarized his revolutionary theory as follows:

> "The Earth is hollow. The Poles, so long sought, are phantoms. There are openings at the northern and southern extremities. In the interior are vast continents, oceans, mountains and rivers. Vegetable and animal life are evident in this New World, and it is probably peopled by races unknown to dwellers on the Earth's surface."

Admiral Byrd's Story

The first publicly available scientific report on the subject was released after Navy Admiral Richard E. Byrd's 1947 flight to the North Pole. According to his diary, instead of going over the pole, he ended up actually entering the Inner Earth through the pole.

In his diary, Byrd describes flying into the hollow interior of the Earth and traveling 1,700 miles over mountains, lakes, rivers, green vegetation and animal life. He tells of seeing monstrous animals resembling the ancient mammoth moving through the underbrush. He eventually found cities and a thriving civilization. He also described an inner Sun inside the Earth.

Later, in January, 1956, Admiral Byrd led another expedition, this time to the Antarctic and the South Pole. In this expedition he claims he and his crew penetrated 2,300 miles into the center of Earth. He states that the North and South Pole are actually two of many openings to the interior of Earth. Ships and planes can actually sail or fly right in.

The US government classified Byrd's diary for a number of years, but it is now available to researchers. An interesting fact relating to all this is that the US government does not allow planes to fly over the poles; all flights are directed to go around the poles.

Colonel Billy Fae Woodard's Story

The story of the hollow Earth gets even more interesting as we hear from more up-to-date sources about it. One of these is a rather intriguing man named Colonel Billy Fae Woodard of the US Air Force. He tells of his years served in the Military's "Area 51" in Nevada from 1971 to 1982. During this time, he says that he visited the hollow interior of the earth six times, going in up to 800 miles deep.

On these visits, he says he was shown by his military superiors the existence of tunnels beneath Area 51. When led into these tunnels, he met several of the underground shuttle operators that were 13 to 14 feet tall. He says he was told that the tunnels traverse the world and were originally built by a species of beings who have existed here for a very long time.

There are also many levels to these tunnels, he reports. The first 15 levels of the Area 51 facility were man-made by the US government, but Levels 16-27 had already been there. He states that the speed of the shuttles is faster than the speed of sound and that they can travel from Area 51 to the main interior of the Earth in less than ten minutes.

Woodard also describes the inner inhabitants of the Hollow Earth (whom he claims he discovered are his direct ancestors). He says that these people always ask permission when working with Nature; they ask the plants for their consent before consuming them or cutting them down, and they also ask Mother Earth before they build in her. They speak telepathically to the many interesting animals that live there.

He says that from what he can tell, there are seven civilizations residing in the Inner Earth, which are all governed by the principles of harmony. They understand and speak all languages of the earth. And their understanding of medical knowledge is phenomenal.

David Wilcock's Insiders' Reports

There are reports from a number of David Wilcock's insider resources who corroborate a lot of Woodard's claims. They confirm that natural cavities do exist inside the earth that have their own source of light, running water, flora and fauna. They explain that in the formation of all watery planets in the universe, hollow cavities are formed below the surface of the crust, containing bacteria capable of giving off natural light.

The insider reports further confirm that these cavities have been utilized by advanced civilizations for millennia to live in safely while watching how the "surface population" works out the dangerous situations it has created. It is estimated that the earth's interior may have over 2,500 different cities that are home to a variety of different types of ETs.

Among these are human-like groups who have lived inside the earth for up to 12 to 18 million years, and look rather similar to us. The "Nordics" are one of these groups, and we are apparently genetically related to these people. At various times in our history they have appeared openly among humans as "Gods", providing our developing species with wisdom and technology to help develop our civilizations.

There is also testimony that during the long history of our planet, numerous other advanced civilizations such as the Atlanteans went underground in order to survive the environmental and political chaos ruling over the surface of our planet. Eventually, they permanently settled into their new subterranean habitat.

Cabal Bases Underground

According to Wilcock's insiders as well as a number of other sources, the Cabal had until recently also tunneled into the Earth for quite some time, creating bases designed to serve as safe places for them to hide when necessary. These bases were built inside huge natural limestone caves in the earth and were often luxurious.

During the process of creating these bases, the Cabal accidentally discovered the homes of other civilizations when they were using tunnel-boring machines to create passageways between their own bases and they would break through into a place where ET beings were living.

There is testimony that the Cabal had a special purpose for creating their underground bases: To provide secure places for them during the aftermath of the full-scale nuclear war they were planning, designed to eliminate much of the surface population.

Their plans for depopulating the earth by poisoning the food and water and creating disease were discussed earlier in this book. However, since humanity's numbers have nonetheless continued to grow in recent decades, the Cabal has had plans for a nuclear war that would accomplish their goal. Even though the benevolent ETs have been making sure this will never happen on earth again, until recently Cabal members were holding onto hope that they could pull this war off.

There was also a vast system of underground "sub-shuttles" that were extremely fast (using ET technology, of course) interlinking these bases. The Cabal's plan was to have enough warning so they could make sure friends and families were safe underground before the nuclear weapons would be detonated.

In these efforts, the Cabal were evidently working in conjunction with a reptilian race known as the "Draco" – who were actually their masters – while these beings were still with us. As we'll see in future chapters, according to several sources the reptilians have now been driven off the planet for good.

It is reported that most of the Cabal bases have been blown up in the last few years by anti-Cabal forces, causing "unexplainable" earthquakes in strange places, such as the Denver Airport and Washington DC.

Interactions between Surface and Inner Earth Populations

Although there has been a commitment to peace between the US secret government and the Inner Earth civilizations, Corey Goode claims that this tenuous relationship has recently become fractured. Elements within the military industrial complex, which had formerly worked with these beings and had entered into treaties with them, are now trying to kill them.

Thus an alliance of the ancient civilizations living inside the planet has formed to resist these new hostile actions. This alliance contacted benevolent interstellar confederations to ask for help in combating the threat they're under. Wilcock describes the aftermath of a meeting between the two alliances. He says that a stunning request was made by the interstellar entities during the meeting.

"The Inner Earth people came out of it quite shell-shocked. They have been asked to reveal themselves to us as part of disclosure. Should the subterranean societies comply with the request, I think we are going to find out that underground bases are much more extensive than we thought and much more ancient."

It is interesting to note that a world symposium recently took place in August 2017 in Garden City, NY, called "Agartha to Humanity", featuring "an Agarthan who has a message for humanity". A report by writer Suzanne Maresca who attended the symposium is both fascinating and uplifting about humanity's future.

Chimera Group Bases

According to Cobra's sources, until recently there was another important civilization living inside the earth. These were the beings he refers to as the "Chimera Group". He tells us they are evidently the "masters" of the Draco and the extremely hostile Archon civilization which will be discussed in the next chapter.

The Chimera came to earth in humanoid physical bodies about 25,000 years ago. Their main strongholds at that time were under Africa, China and Tibet. They had no direct contact with the surface civilization until the early 20th century. The Chimera group had their own network of underground bases until those were recently cleared out by the Resistance Movement (which you can read about in Chapter 13).

ETs under the Ice in Antarctica

One of the most intriguing pieces of news about civilizations living inside of the Earth recently emerged at the end of 2016, mainly through Corey Goode, who was invited to see spectacular developments happening in Antarctica. What he and now others are reporting is that a number of different governments, including the US, have been excavating on this frozen continent for several decades and have discovered amazing phenomena there. What they found was an extremely ancient series of cities flash-frozen deep under the ice-shelf. And, believe it or not, there are also civilizations that are still alive and well nearby living within the earth.

Goode describes the cavern area he was taken to in which inhabitants were still living, saying it was gigantic. "It was like New York, or Manhattan, under the ground." There were natural pillars inside the cavern; and inside these pillars was "what looked like a bunch of condos". He says the people of this civilization trace their lineage back 18 million years.

Artifacts and Frozen Bodies

Nearby and in lower layers which teams from several countries have excavated, there are many types of ruins and artifacts strewn across the continent. These have been discovered through the use of steam blowers that melt the ice very effectively. Many square miles of ruins have been detected, with only a small percentage that has actually been excavated thus far.

Within the stunning array of ruins they have also found flash-frozen pre-historic animals and inhabitants who apparently had been killed in a major catastrophe of some kind. There are trees, plants and wildlife frozen in place, like they were put on pause. There are also three massive ships that apparently crash-landed on earth that have been jokingly called by those working with the ruins as "the Pinta, the Nina and the Santa Maria."

A great number of mummified bodies were also found preserved in the ice. These have been identified as the ET race known as the "Fallen Angels" or "Pre-Adamites" described in the next chapter. They have elongated heads and strangely proportioned bodies that scientists say were not designed for Earth's gravity and atmospheric pressure.

It is believed that this Pre-Adamite group came here from another planet in our solar system that was no longer hospitable. They evidently arrived with little technology due to the dire situation they found themselves in and wanted to take advantage of ruins and technology left earlier in Antarctica by an ET race known as the "Ancient Builder Race". There is also evidence that soon after they arrived here they began genetic experiments to create hybrids of their species and the developing human population. Bodies of some of these hybrids have been found along with those of the Pre-Adamites.

Although it appears that there was already some ice on Antarctica when the Pre-Adamites arrived, the continent was in a different geographical position than it is today – much closer to the equator.

Antarctica – Ruins of Atlantis?

There are many claims that what is being uncovered in Antarctica are the remains of Atlantis that have finally been discovered, just as the "sleeping prophet" Edgar Cayce claimed back in the early 1900s they would be. Actually, nearly every culture of the world has legends of this ancient civilization and of the Great Flood that took it down about 12,000 years ago. For over two hundred years researchers have searched for the remains of Atlantis, excavating some forty different locations seeking to match them with the description given by Plato 2300 years ago.

According to Wilcock's insiders, what we now see as Antarctica is indeed where the lost land of Atlantis is to be found. Geologists suggest that the earth shifted on its rotational axis at some point, perhaps due to a nuclear war, and the water that inundated the continent quickly flash-froze into a gigantic ice shelf.

Because of this great flood, the hybrid survivors of the Pre-Adamite race who were living on other continents at the time completely lost access to their ancient cities on Atlantis. But they evidently then began to breed with the human populations in the regions they were stationed in at the time of the flood. One major faction of the Pre-Adamite groups remained in the Americas, while the other survived in Europe, Africa and Asia.

Draco in Antarctica

Other intel about Antarctica is from insider William Tomkins who, as described earlier, had the job of interviewing captured German spies during WW II. He tells us that these spies confirmed that the Nazis were already excavating in Antarctica at that time, back in the 1930s.

He reports that they came in contact at that time with a violent, aggressive race with both humanoid and reptilian features, known as the Draco. Indeed, there are many reporting now that during the war, the Draco made a deal with Hitler and the Nazis to work together. In particular, the Draco were consultants in building space craft for the Germans. This certainly adds an interesting piece to the whole WW II drama.

While the Draco have had central bases of operations in several different places in our solar system, a primary one was in Antarctica in a vast under-ice facility. As we will see in the next chapter, the Draco have posed a huge problem not only on the earth but also in our whole region of the galaxy. In a future chapter, you'll read how the US forces have recently been destroying the Draco facilities.

Recent Big-Wig Visitors to Antarctica

In late 2016, right after the US presidential election, a big flurry of intel began coming out about various world political and religious leaders who were being taken down to Antarctica. This was reportedly to show them the new archeological finds that were being uncovered.

US top diplomat John Kerry actually flew there on Election Day. Buzz Aldrin visited the ruins as well, although something caused him to fall ill and leave the area before he was scheduled to. It is rumored that a number of other top political leaders were invited, as well. Goode describes the tours for these people as a "cosmic adult Disneyland."

ETs inside the Earth – References

Inner Earth Civilizations
1. "David Wilcock: Inner Earth Civilizations May Soon Reveal Themselves to the World". http://humansarefree.com/2015/12/david-wilcock-inner-earth-civilizations.html
2. Woodard, Billy Fae. http://www.ourhollowearth.com/ColBillieFayeWoodard.htm
3. Zorra. http://www.blogtalkradio.com/zorraofhollowearth/2016/11/19/zorra-of-hollow-earth-1

Agartha
1. Agartha World Symposium. "Agartha to Humanity World Symposium: Ambassador of the Inner Earth Kingdom of Agartha". https://www.agarthaworldsymposium.com/
2. Galactic Federation Council of Sirius: The Realm of Agartha". http://www.thenewearth.org/GalacticFederationArchive.html
3. Maresca, Suzanne. "Everybody was Someone You Could Talk to". http://goldenageofgaia.com/2017/08/25/everyone-was-someone-you-could-talk-to-first-agarthan-update/
4. Stone, Joshua David. "The Inner Earth and Realm of Agartha". http://www.thenewearth.org/InnerEarth.html

Metaphysical Sources
1. Jones, Aurelia Louise. *Telos.* https://www.amazon.com/Revelations-New-Lemuria-TELOS-Vol/dp/0970090242/ref=sr_1_1?s=books&ie=UTF8&qid=1503038001&sr=1-1&keywords=telos
2. Nidle, Sheldan. "Inner Earth – Sheldan Nidle". https://www.youtube.com/watch?v=hSgKbCrwq3o
3. Robbins, Dianne. "TELOS - A Subterranean City beneath Mt. Shasta". https://www.diannerobbins.com/telos.html

Explorers of Inner Earth
1. Reed, William. *Phantom of the Poles.* https://www.amazon.com/s/ref=nb_sb_noss?url=search-alias%3Dstripbooks&field-keywords=Phantom+of+the+Poles
2. Goerler, Raimund E. "Richard E. Byrd And The North Pole Flight Of 1926: Fact, Fiction As Fact, And Interpretation". file:///C:/Users/Owner/Downloads/proc98363.pdf
3. Woodard Billy Fae. Area 51 Revealed-The Col. Billie Faye Woodard Story". https://www.youtube.com/watch?v=8jFa-KrZVck

Cabal Bases Underground
1. Wilcock, David and Goode, Corey. "Cosmic Disclosure: Disclosure and the Secret Underground War".
https://spherebeingalliance.com/blog/transcript-cosmic-disclosure-disclosure-and-the-secret-underground-war.html
2. Wilcock, David. *Ascension Mysteries,* pg. 91, 159, 328-30.
https://www.amazon.com/Ascension-Mysteries-Revealing-Cosmic-Between-ebook/dp/B0191ZL2EC

Inner Earth Alliance
1. Wilcock, David. "Inner Earth Alliance".
http://contactinthedesert.com/dwilcock/
2. http://humansarefree.com/2011/05/hollow-earth-agartha-complete.html

Chimera Group Bases
1. Cobra. "Fall of the Chimera".
http://2012portal.blogspot.com/2014/07/fall-of-chimera.html
Antarctica
2. Goode, Corey. "ETs and Inner Earth Beings".
https://spherebeingalliance.com/blog/transcript-ets-and-inner-earth-beings.html
3. Wilcock, David. Endgame 2. http://divinecosmos.com/start-here/davids-blog/1209-endgame-pt-2

Cosmic Battle between the
Dark and the Light

Chapter 11

Untold History of Humanity and ETs

So it's one thing to accept that ET races are here now, in our skies, on the Earth and within the Earth. But it's another to truly understand that many of them may have lived here on Earth even before human beings were here. Indeed, numerous races of ETs have visited the Earth in the past, creating large civilizations and greatly impacting the human race over long periods of time.

In David Wilcock's recent book, *The Ascension Mysteries: Revealing the Cosmic Battle between Good and Evil,* he tells the long tale of humanity's struggle with ET races who periodically landed on Earth and essentially set themselves up as gods over the human race and in many ways enslaved them. He indicates that some of those races may still be here with us, just more hidden and disguised, and that they continue to exert their control through the Cabal.

Our ET Ancestry

In fact, Wilcock reports that many of the invading ET groups interbred with humans over time, and others contributed their DNA to the human structure – which means that ETs are actually among our ancestors. This becomes clear in reading the testimony from Wilcock's insiders, as well as information from a number of other sources. Indeed, what we understand about who we are as human beings is not only drastically limited, but in many ways all wrong.

We come to realize that our education about our history and our ancestors has in many ways been controlled – that there's a spin on everything we learn about humanity, designed essentially to keep us uninformed and disempowered. We have not learned, for example, how very old the human race is or how our race was conceived of to begin with.

Not everyone claiming information on the subject agrees about the details, but many of them describe similar races of ETs that are part of our history and played a role in our genetic makeup.

ET Origins

First, there are a number of authors, such as Dolores Cannon, Michael Tellinger and Sheldan Nidle, who offer their understanding of our ET origins. They speak about our true ancestors from way back, telling us they came from a number of different star systems, including the Pleiades, Sirius, Orion, Andromeda and Arcturus. The Pleiadians evidently had a large role in originally creating the homo sapiens species, the humans we are today.

According to these sources, the beings from these star systems are actually our "galactic family" who originally created – and then tinkered with – our DNA. Some of these ETs apparently lovingly offered more advanced DNA to help us along in our evolution as a species, and some others very deliberately made adjustments to dumb us down to be more pliable for their own plans for domination.

ETs Have Shaped Us

The fact that our link with our Galactic Family goes back far into our history is also known to certain scientists and historians but kept from the general public. Much of the rest of the information in this chapter is drawn from David Wilcock's intel from his many insiders and is corroborated by Corey Goode, who learned about the true history of the human race through his work in the secret space program on the moon.

According to these sources, ETs have been with us since the beginning and have shaped us physiologically, culturally, and psychologically. Insiders have learned this from certain ETs themselves, as well as from humans who have been in the programs.

It is especially important at this time to realize that the human race hasn't had a smooth and even path of evolution. There were a number of huge galactic battles that took place long ago in which the young human race got caught in the middle. These events powerfully shaped our evolution. And some of what occurred with certain hostile races is very relevant to the Cabal-controlled situation we find ourselves in today.

Ancient Builder Race

According to Wilcock's information, the first race that visited earth in ancient times has been called the "Ancient Builder Race" and is sometimes referred to as "the Guardians". A channeled work called "The Law of One" states that the Ancient Builder Race first originated on Venus when that planet was still earth-like about 2.6 billion years ago.

Wilcock's sources say that these beings were a very positive race that lived harmoniously with all races here at the time. They also had the technology to expand and explore all around the galaxy without any interference.

The Guardians brought many advanced ideas and technology to move humanity along in evolution. Humans saw them as gods who had arrived out of the sky. It is said that this race created a protective grid for our local cluster of planets in order to prevent negative races from being able to come here. And then at some point, after reaching a stunning apex of civilization, they mysteriously vanished.

The oldest artifacts on earth are attributed to the Ancient Builder Race. The ruins of hundreds of their cities have also been found inside the Earth, containing large buildings, pyramids and obelisks. Apparently these beings were much larger than humans and were feline-featured. Many ancient cultures world-wide show these beings in their art. The ruins of this civilization are apparently at least five million years old.

After leaving the solar system long ago, they have been returning recently and are now playing a role, along with other benevolent ETs, to help humanity evolve into freedom. These benevolent ETs evidently also want us to know that they are our ancestors and that we share much of the same DNA; ours simply is not yet activated as much as theirs is.

Genetic Farmers

Another early group to visit earth and leave their DNA with the human race has been dubbed the "Genetic Farmers". These were groups who saw the Earth as a jewel in the universe, as it supports a great deal more plant and animal life than most planets do. The Earth apparently has what it takes to support a high diversity of life. Almost any life form from anywhere can be dropped off here and survive.

The Genetic Farmers took sections of DNA from all over the galaxy and carefully spliced it into humans on earth. Some of the groups did this intending to optimize humans for evolution. Others did it for more selfish reasons to control them.

Beings from Super Earth

Another group of ETs that apparently helped to form the human race was a giant race referred to as "Beings from Super Earth". The large earth-like planet they originally lived on has also been called "Maldek". Positioned between Mars and Jupiter, it was a watery livable place, with an earth-like atmosphere. Mars at the time was one of its moons.

We're told that a huge catastrophe destroyed Maldek about 500,000 yrs ago. This event was also responsible for making Mars inhabitable. The survivors of the cataclysm migrated to Earth. With them, they brought advanced technology, including internet type technology (which apparently is a very common development in advanced civilizations). They also brought warlike ideas and values.

The really important thing that happened with the eruption of the Super Earth planet, however, is that it destroyed the protective grid the Ancient Builder Race had put in place to protect this area of the solar system against invasions by hostile ET races. The destruction of this grid allowed for a massive immigration of groups that had previously been excluded – and for them to land on Earth.

The Draco

The most impactful of the ET races that inhabited the Earth are those referred to as "Draco", beings who arrived about 375,000 years ago from the Orion star system. They were composed of six different large reptilian-humanoid species who thrived on domination and control.

When they arrived on Earth, they made it clear they considered themselves the "master race" among the humans. Eventually they genetically intermingled with humanity, and in essence, created the ancestors of the present Cabal – a lineage of hybrids to help them in their plan to rule the earth and enslave humanity. So ironically, the human beings who have been born over the centuries into the bloodline of the Cabal have themselves been slaves to these Draco beings.

Over the millennia, the Reptilians have from time to time been expelled from the Earth by groups of benevolent ETs. But they've tended to come back during times of weakness, such as after a cataclysm. The latest earth cataclysm happened about 12,800 years ago, destroying the civilization known as Atlantis. Certain groups of Atlanteans had been able to keep the Reptilians in check, but after the fall of this civilization, the Reptilians came back in force – and, until very recently, we've been dealing with them ever since.

The Anunnaki

Another group of ETs that much is written about are the Anunnaki. According to author, scientist and explorer, Michael Tellinger, this race arrived on earth about 200,000 years ago. They were evidently sent to earth from a planet called Nibiru in search of life-saving gold. They created a group of humans whom they used as a slave race to mine gold.

There is a lot on the internet about this race, much of it negative. But we've learned that there are actually two groups of Anunnaki – one group that became very negative while on earth, and the other who refused to be part of what the first group was doing and subsequently left. We are told that this positive group is now back, along with others to assist humanity to ascend into higher consciousness.

The Fallen Angels

Yet another group of ETs arrived here about 55,000 years ago called the "Fallen Angels" or the "Pre-Adamites", remains of which were recently found under the ice in Antarctica, as mentioned in the last chapter. These beings were tall humanoid giants with elongated heads. Very intelligent, with advanced technology, they were another race to set themselves up among humans as gods. They too interbred with humans, and so as time went on, they lost some of their height.

Their initial civilization was destroyed 50,000 years ago, but they then arose again in the civilization known as Atlantis. They continued on into ancient Egypt, becoming the Egyptian priesthood and entered the lineage of pharaohs. We're told there is a huge treasure trove of artifacts created by these people under the sands of the Egyptian desert, including libraries, technology, and spacecraft.

You can see images of them with their elongated heads in much of the Egyptian art of that period, as well as in that of other civilizations. These images are not just a stylized depiction of people; their skulls actually looked that way.

We also know that people with that kind of skull were still living as late as the 14th Century, seen in a painting of a European Prince Leonello and Princess D'Este who clearly have elongated heads. Actually, these type skulls have been found all over the planet in graves of elites who lived throughout history in Europe, Russia, Peru, and Siberia.

Recently, in late 2017, a mummy with an elongated head was discovered in Peru. She was named the "Nazca Mummy" and received a lot of attention in the media and in science. Subsequently two more mummies like Nazca were discovered. They all have three-fingered hands.

What's very interesting are reports that there are apparently people with elongated skulls who still exist today. Many are in the Vatican and are known to some as "Homo Capensis". An insider from the World Bank stated:

> "There is a second species on this planet...They are not ETs. And they are very distinct from homo sapiens. One of the places they've been hiding is the Vatican. That's why the Vatican men are wearing those miters."

So, according to insider sources, there is evidence that ETs and their off-spring are still living among us today. And, very importantly, these beings are still in a position, after many thousands of years, with the potential to dominate the human race.

Thankfully there is, at long last, news from these sources that the battle between the Dark and the Light is now being won by the Light Forces. And the condition of domination of the human race will finally be coming to an end.

Untold History of Humanity – References

ET History on Earth
1. Frye, Megan. "Aliens: Earth's Future is Not Written in Stone".
http://prepareforchange.net/aliens-earths-future-not-written-stone/
2. Nidle, Sheldon. http://sananda.website/the-galactic-federation-of-light-via-sheldan-nidle-june-27th-2017/
3. Tellinger, Michael. http://www.michaeltellinger.com/
4. Wilcock, David. *Ascension Mysteries*, pg. 362.
https://www.amazon.com/s/ref=nb_sb_noss?url=search-alias%3Dstripbooks&field-keywords=wilcock+ascension+mysteries

ET Origins & Ancestry
1. Tellinger, Michael. "Full Episode: Hidden Origins with Michael Tellinger (Season 1, Episode 1) on Gaia".
https://www.youtube.com/watch?v=f0zBv-DrXbk
2. Wilcock, David. *Ascension Mysteries.*
https://www.amazon.com/s/ref=nb_sb_noss?url=search-alias%3Dstripbooks&field-keywords=wilcock+ascension+mysteries

Ancient Builder Race
Wilcock, David. *Ascension Mysteries*, pg. 381.
https://www.amazon.com/s/ref=nb_sb_noss?url=search-alias%3Dstripbooks&field-keywords=wilcock+ascension+mysteries

Genetic Farmers
Wilcock, David. *Ascension Mysteries*, pg. 430.
https://www.amazon.com/s/ref=nb_sb_noss?url=search-alias%3Dstripbooks&field-keywords=wilcock+ascension+mysteries

Beings from Super Earth
Wilcock, David. *Ascension Mysteries*, 388.
https://www.amazon.com/s/ref=nb_sb_noss?url=search-alias%3Dstripbooks&field-keywords=wilcock+ascension+mysteries

Draco
1. Goode, Corey. "ETs and Inner Earth Beings".
https://spherebeingalliance.com/blog/transcript-ets-and-inner-earth-beings.html
2. Wilcock, David. *Ascension Mysteries*, 431,446.
https://www.amazon.com/s/ref=nb_sb_noss?url=search-alias%3Dstripbooks&field-keywords=wilcock+ascension+mysteries

Anunnaki
1. Tellinger, Michael. "New Hidden Anunnaki Origins 2016".
https://www.youtube.com/watch?v=HnbYAYkKng0

2. The Ancient Aliens website. "Anunnaki, Creation of Humans".
http://www.theancientaliens.com/creation-of-humans

Fallen Angels
Wilcock, David. *Ascension Mysteries,* pg. 411
https://www.amazon.com/s/ref=nb_sb_noss?url=search-
alias%3Dstripbooks&field-keywords=wilcock+ascension+mysteries

Nazca Mummy
1. Wallia, Arjun. "Potential Alien Body Unearthed In Nazca, Peru. A Species
Unlike Anything Found In The Fossil Record?" - https://goo.gl/pRwTTU
2. Gaia website. "Unearthing Nazca". https://goo.gl/N3YFHH

Chapter 12

Earth in Quarantine

This chapter offers a somewhat different story from that told by David Wilcock and Corey Goode about the cosmic battle between dark and light forces and how humans have been greatly impacted by it. It is based on information given by a whistle-blower known as "Cobra", a man who calls himself a "Pleiadian contactee", who has been working for over 35 years with the "Resistance Movement" operated by ET beings involved in resisting the Dark Forces.

He is becoming increasingly well-known to thousands around the world, many of whom who have joined in mass meditations he has orchestrated to accelerate the liberation of the planet. On August 21, 2107, over a quarter million people participated in one of these meditations, which he reported had powerful results.

Cobra's reports focus on two groups of ETs known as the "Chimera Group" and the "Archons" who both arrived on earth about 25,000 years ago and together essentially took humanity hostage in a number of different ways. They are evidently the group that created the Draco and reptilian races Wilcock and Goode speak about.

Cobra states that the Chimera Group members are incarnated physically in human hybrid form on and within the earth and have infiltrated the vast majority of military bases around the world, many belonging to the US, as well as many of the financial, religious and political structures in the world. The Archons exist in both physical and non-physical bodies and basically exert control over humanity from other dimensions. I will refer to both these groups together as the "Dark Forces".

Because Cobra's story has such a complex depth and a multiplicity of dimensions that can't be described in its fullness through words, the story is told simply, as a fantasy tale might be. Or like the movie "Star Wars" depicted.

But in reading the story perhaps you can just absorb it into your consciousness, allowing it to awaken deep unconscious memories that may reside within you. If you have related to other material in this book so far, you likely do have these memories deep within you.

The Fatal Experiment

The story begins with the description of the Archons and the Chimera as a group of high-density, trans-dimensional beings originating in the Andromeda and Orion star systems. These beings chose at one point to plunge into an "experiment", essentially asking: "What would happen if we disconnected from Source?"

Unfortunately, their experiment failed, in that once they'd disconnected themselves from Source, they couldn't find a way to connect back. And so they fell into darkness without access to the Light from the Source of all being. In that state of disconnection, they decided to go out to conquer the galaxy. They began roaming the cosmos, conquering and destroying many worlds for millions of years, creating a massive empire they alone controlled. During this time, they created the draconian and reptilian slave races through genetic engineering.

In other words, what resulted from this experiment is what we call today "darkness" or "evil".

At some point, benevolent Light Forces from all over the universe began gathering to take action to prevent what the Dark Forces were doing. They began pursuing them, in an effort to free planets and other ET races the Dark Forces had conquered. This was the beginning of the Galactic Wars.

Humanity in Isolation

Eventually, about 25,000 years ago, having been chased out of every other star system in the cosmos, the Dark Forces had to concentrate themselves in one small part of the universe. They ended up in our planetary system, and eventually on earth, using this planet as their last stronghold.

Upon arrival, they took humanity hostage and declared a quarantine whereby no ships could land without pre-approval. They threatened nuclear war if the Light Forces were to attempt to come in. With their highly advanced technology, they quickly surrounded the earth with a scalar electromagnetic grid known as "the Veil" around the earth, securing it in quarantine. This effectively prevented positive ET contact and thus isolated humanity.

The vast majority of the benevolent ETs who were already on the earth retreated underground and developed cities of light connected by tunnels, trains, and the alliance known as the Agarthan Network. From this position, they focused as well as they could on maintaining the balance of light on earth, helping to stabilize it.

But, because the Dark Forces had such a tight control over the people living on the surface, it was too dangerous for the Agarthans to come to the surface to help. Nonetheless, there were various people who found their way into the earth where the Agarthans lived, such as the Mayans, Hopis, Anasazis, Incas, Templars, and Aztecs. Much of the Inca gold and the Templar gold that legends speak of was taken underground for safe-keeping at that time.

Control of Human Consciousness

Meanwhile, the Archons, having assumed control of humanity on the inner planes, furthered their domination over humans by designing ways to hijack the karmic wheel and the reincarnation process of the human race and established themselves on the etheric and astral planes as the "Lords of Karma". In doing this, they were able to determine to a large degree our life circumstances when we incarnated into a new body. They've essentially considered humanity their "herd" that is here for them to feed off of, so they've kept us on the wheel of karma, stifling our opportunities for attaining liberation from it.

As we saw in earlier chapters, the Dark Force beings existing in physical form began breeding with certain humans and also recruiting others as their "minions", thus creating the Cabal and Illuminati bloodlines which would serve to keep humanity in line. In the past, there were the royal bloodline sovereigns and priests who acted in this role. Today these royal bloodlines are mainly hidden in our political, military, religious and corporate structures.

The energetic Veil technology still in operation today also includes the placement of implants in our etheric bodies, designed to suppress the consciousness and prevent spiritual awakening.

The technology also helps prevent us from being able to form a coherent telepathic consciousness with each other, whereby we could become dangerous to them. They also use AI and spacecraft to monitor our thoughts and steer us away from information that would help us grow spiritually.

The Fall of Consciousness

So this is a rather dark version of the story of the Fall of Consciousness into the extremely dense Third Dimension with all its inherent distortions and anomalies causing immense suffering. We have been living in this fallen state for these last 25,000 years or so.

It's important to recognize what this fallen state of humanity has entailed, as we tend to simply take the aspects of our fallen state for granted since it's all we've known for so long. We no longer have reference points of what is like to be living in a civilization of beings who are not existing as a fallen race.

The "fallen" state involves the fact that life is generally fraught with difficulty. The human condition is dominated by the struggle for survival, and much of humanity lives in poverty, barely maintaining the necessities of life. Most of our time and energy go into obtaining food and shelter. Additionally, we experience illness, difficult aging, suffering, and physical death.

Relationships on earth often bring deep disappointment, sorrow and heartache, and many people are alone, abused, or emotionally lost. Any sense of true fulfillment is rare and usually fleeting. All but a few exist in a state of separation from the Divine and forgetfulness of their own divine nature.

The fallen state of our planet also means that just about all of our institutions are corrupt, and that no matter how hard we try to change or replace them, corruption always seems to take over again. Most countries are unable to live in peace with one another; and despite all the efforts of those desiring peace throughout history, we still fight and kill one another. And always the innocent suffer.

Most of us generally accept that this is just "how life is". It's what we're brought up to believe, what we learn in school. Life is struggle, you have to work to survive (unless you're one of the very few fortunate ones), and life always has sorrow woven through it.

Unbeknownst to most people, in the many unfallen civilizations existing throughout the universe, none of this is true. What we generally experience in life here is due to our fallen state as a species. It's a result of the fact that we live behind massive energetic barriers which keep the Light of the Creator from us.

Although all of this is at long last changing at a fairly rapid pace, we are still somewhat at the effect of these controlling forces that were set in place thousands of years ago.

What does This All Mean?

Think about all this for a moment. We're being told that we are a race enslaved by other hostile races and have been for thousands of years. If this is all or even just somewhat true, consider what it might mean, not only for humanity as a whole, but for each of us as individuals.

If, indeed, we have been held as hostages in quarantine, if we have had implants inserted into our consciousness to control us with negative programming that holds back our awakening to Source, and if we have been incarnating over and over again through a karmic system designed to keep us unaware of who we really are – what does this all mean about us?

Have you ever wondered why, no matter how much awakening and healing work you've done, there always seems to be more to move through? And why you never get free of your feelings of self-doubt and self-judgment, no matter how much love and respect you develop for yourself?

Do you ever get the sense you're somehow being "interfered" with? That there are forces messing with you, preventing you from making the breakthroughs you long for and work toward? If so, have you just decided that there must be something wrong or flawed about you, and that you just have to do more "work" on yourself?

Have you ever wondered about your superego, the inner critic that always seems to be making you wrong in some way, no matter what you do? Why is there something within you that is always tripping you up with self-judgment, guilt, shame and self-hatred? Does it ever feel like this is not a natural part of you?

Could this story of the Dark Forces and humanity perhaps bring some clarity to these questions? Feel into this possibility. What could this mean for you if it is true?

Awakening to the Truth

Although, in truth, we have definitely been victimized as an entire race, this isn't to say we need to feel or act like victims. What this tells us is yes, we have had the cards stacked against us in many ways that have been totally unseen and out of our reach. But we can now wake up to this fact.

Once we awaken to the truth about the negative forces that have been interfering with our consciousness, we can begin to discover our innate power as Light Beings to burst free, past these age-old restraints, and awaken to who we really are. As they say, the Truth can set us free.

As we will see in the following chapter, we are getting a great deal of help from many who are working to liberate us from these negative forces that have held us hostage. However, we must still do our own work to free ourselves of the old negative third-dimensional habit patterns we hold – all the beliefs around separation, all judgment, all the feelings of fear, shame, guilt, hatred, and despair. In other words, it's essential that we continue doing our healing and clearing work on ourselves. As sovereign beings, we are responsible for ourselves and our individual ascension process.

At the same time, we need to stay aware of how the negative forces continue to affect us on the inner planes. In particular, in order to create divisions and conflicts, the Archons are still exerting pressure on psychological weak spots of people who are attempting to be a positive force for humanity and the Earth. This serves the Archons' purpose to diffuse our positive alignment into quarrels and divisions with each other and away from our focused intent on freeing ourselves from the control of the negative forces.

In general, we need to keep ourselves surrounded with protective light, especially when we are in public or when we are involved in projects aimed to bring greater light to the planet. It's extremely helpful to develop a daily practice of some form of meditation in which we call forth the Light for protection.

Group meditations for the planet's liberation and awakening are also very powerful, along with intentional and vivid visualizing of a planet freed of domination. We've been told that a certain percentage of humanity needs to awaken to the truth of what's happening with the Dark Forces, at least to some degree, to reach a critical mass that will help precipitate the "Event", a planetary awakening (which will be described in Chapter 16). Meditations focused on global awakening accelerate this process.

What can perhaps make the most impactful difference in our personal lives is simply realizing that any negative states of consciousness we may fall into are mainly habitual, artificially-induced programmings and not part of the original human design. Realizing that these are not a natural part of us can help us enormously to let go of them much more quickly. They are simply "Archonic control patterns" that we have taken on – which, with understanding, we can release.

Dwindling Dark Forces

The good news is that the Archons and Chimera Group members are being removed from planet earth at this time. As you will see in the following chapters, thanks to several different Light Alliances, the dark structure is now, at long last, falling apart. The timing is finally right. The earth has entered a part of the galaxy in which this is now both possible and likely. Humanity has made leaps in consciousness before during these historical cosmic passages through space, and it can do that again this time – especially with help from the Light Alliances.

An interesting note that Cobra makes is that the Light Alliances have been finding the task of liberating humanity a much harder one than they'd originally expected, and so it's been taking longer than they'd planned. But we're assured that the task is finally now being completed at this point.

Basically only a small number of Dark Force members are left, and they are panicked at this point with the Light Forces now arriving in full force, in concert with high-frequency energies flowing from the central sun onto the planet. They know their days are numbered.

Responding to the Material

You have now read two versions of the same basic story about humanity's history with ET races, complete with on-going cosmic battling. The details are somewhat different, the emphasis in each is different; but the assertion that humanity has essentially been enslaved for a very long time is the same. This understanding can be deeply unsettling.

I suggest you take time to tune in to see how the information may be affecting you emotionally. Be kind to yourself. It can be a lot to take in all that it implies. Even though the Light Forces are now winning the epic battle with the Dark, knowing that as a Lightworker you have likely been personally involved in this battle for eons of time can initially create a profound heaviness in your heart.

In particular, you may experience deep grief and rage arising from your unconscious about how long this whole process of bringing the Light back to the Earth has taken. Become aware of how ancient you probably are. How many eons you have lived through the cosmic wars. You may remember who you originally were – someone who way back in time was already attempting to fulfill your mission. Taking all this in may also have an effect on your entire belief system and cosmology, challenging long-held concepts about what is real.

As difficult as it may be to consider all this, it is important to do so. In order to release any acute pain that may be hidden within you, it is necessary for it to first come into conscious awareness, so it can be acknowledged and experienced – and then released.

It's not necessary to relive every incident or harmful situation you've experienced throughout the millennia. But it can be helpful to look at your current life and the imbalances in it - the big stories, the big heartaches, the big frustrations - and understand that they likely reflect an overall pattern you have carried with you for many thousands of years. Understand that these are times in which all old painful memories are arising in order to be released – and that it's time to finally meet them -- and let them go.

As it all eventually settles within you, you may begin to feel a sense of deeper peace and empowerment than you've ever felt before. Taking in the Truth eventually tends to have this effect on us.

Earth in Quarantine – References

1. Calise, Greg. "The Enslavement of Souls and the Archon Gate Keepers". http://humansarefree.com/2017/07/the-enslavement-of-souls-and-archon.html
2. Cobra. "Earth in Quarantine". http://prepareforchange.net/earth-quarantine-last-26000-years/
3. Cobra. "Fall of the Chimera". http://2012portal.blogspot.com/2014/07/fall-of-chimera.html
4. Coloborama. "Return to Light – Cobra". http://2012portal.blogspot.pt/2017/07/return-to-light.html
5. Morgan, Edward. "The Chimera Group—the Root of All Evil". http://prepareforchange.net/2017/09/03/the-chimera-group-the-root-of-all-evil/
Cobra's Website: The Portal. http://2012portal.blogspot.com/

Victory of the Light Forces

Chapter 13

Light Force Alliances

Considering all these stories about our history and battles with the Dark Forces, along with all the secrecy that exists about them, it can seem impossible that anything could turn all of it around. So many people in the past have attempted to bring down the Dark Forces in all their various forms and to reveal the secrets being held from us – and yet nothing has ever really changed. Why would anything be different now?

The truth is these times we are currently living in *are* different. As we've seen, there are now very powerful alliances that have formed and are busy bringing down both the Cabal and the dark ETs in order to release us from their control. Many reports are now confirming that the epic cosmic battle between the Dark and the Light is now coming to an end. And, from what we hear from multiple sources, the Light Forces, which greatly outnumber the Dark Forces at this point, are finally winning.

Basically there are three alliances within these Light Forces that have been working closely together behind the scenes to release us from the powers that have controlled us.

The Earth Alliance

The first group has been called the "Earth Alliance". This consists, first of all, of a variety of whistle-blowers, researchers and investigators, including all the ones I've mentioned so far and others to be named in Chapter 15 who are working toward disclosure.

It also includes many people within the government – especially within the intelligence agencies, including the FBI, the CIA and the

Department of Defense – all of whom are dedicated to disclosure and to bringing the Cabal to justice. This is world-wide; most countries know about the Cabal and have factions in their governments fighting against it. Some say that even Russian Prime Minister Putin is on board with this goal – even that he is working with benevolent ETs who are assisting him.

The Earth Alliance contains many who have incarnated to fill positions of power specifically in order to help transform the planet. They will be in the background when the predicted mass arrests of the Cabal begin to happen. Some of them are ex-Cabal members who have become courageous whistle-blowers.

There are also people inside the police forces who have the same mission to take down the Cabal and who will be the ones making the arrests around the world. It is said that the arrests of the most powerful Cabal members will take place in a coordinated manner at the same time everywhere.

In addition, although perhaps surprising to some, there are a great many inside the military all around the world who have also joined the ranks of the Light Forces, especially within the US, Russia and China military. We're told that the US forces now have the capability of shooting down the Cabal's orbiting craft and of deactivating its technology, when necessary.

Marines Fighting the Draco

As noted earlier, the US military forces are also being used to take out underground bases the Cabal has created as places to hide. An interesting story from insiders in early 2017 reported that groups of Marines that were being sent into these underground bases where hold-outs of the Cabal were hiding. They had instructions to blast them out of hiding, if necessary. These Cabal members had previously been given the ultimatum to surrender by a certain date – or they'd be taken out. But they had chosen to go underground into their bases.

So a group of Marines was sent to one of these underground bases, to break through the concrete and cut through the steel, with instructions to give all those inside one last opportunity to surrender. If this didn't happen, they were to kill everyone in the entire base. These Marines were Special Forces – tough, well-trained men. Unfortunately, however, they had not been briefed on anything non-terrestrial they might encounter. They thought they were just going in to clean out a bunch of criminals.

Much to their shock after they had breached the base, they found themselves face-to-face with huge Reptilians doing battle with them. (These, as you'll recall, are the Draco that were still in residence inside the Earth in various places). As Corey Goode tells the story: "A lot of these Marines are, you know, Southern boys; and the next thing you know, they're fighting something that looks like the Devil according to their belief systems." As might be expected, although the Marines were apparently successful in their task to destroy all those who had been hiding in the base, many of them were so traumatized by the ETs, they were unable to function after this battle.

Galactic Alliance

The second alliance involved in freeing humanity is a many-faceted cosmic alliance described in previous chapters, sometimes referred to as the "Galactic Confederation", or at times as the "Sky Crew".

This group reportedly includes a multitude of ET beings from thousands of different star systems. All are beings who have reached a certain level of advanced evolutionary development and have come together, dedicated to assist other races who live in this part of the universe to live in peace and harmony. Within this group also are members of the Angelics and certain Ascended Masters. At this point, as we've seen, these forces have apparently liberated all other solar systems and planets from the Dark Forces; the Earth is the last place that needs to be set free.

These benevolent ET forces are not only here to help liberate us. They are also concerned about humanity's evolutionary development, knowing our race needs help in order to take advantage of the "Shift of the Ages" we are now entering and they wish to assist us through our ascension process – an opportunity that only occurs every 26,000 years or so. They are also concerned about their own civilizations which have been affected by the nuclear warfare humanity has engaged in during the last century.

Visionary and author, Gordon Asher Davidson, offers another piece of interesting information that further confirms the galactic light forces' concern about the Earth:

"Because Earth is one of the chakras of the living
being of our solar system, it affects the larger whole
and has long been holding back the evolution of our
solar system."

He adds that the "Light Guardians" of our planet had originally
been aware of the ET predators on the Earth but had made a
decision that these beings "would be allowed to remain to become
part of Earth's evolutionary process, so that humanity would have
the ability to choose between light and darkness." He adds,
however, that a cosmic decree was finally made following the
events of 9/11 to offset the power of the dark ET-run Cabal and
have them removed by the galactic forces.

He confirms that we are now being given active help from
galactic sources and spiritual masters to support the resolution of
Earth's crisis and our movement into an entirely new civilization of
light and love.

Cobra focuses in detail on the take-down of the Dark Forces. He
tells us that the Galactic Confederation he is in touch with is a
particular alliance that oversees the evolution in this Galaxy and
that they have been gathering around this planet, cloaked, for some
time now in their motherships.

Many of these ships use fifth-dimensional vortexes of light to
balance the energy grid around the planet. They are also working
to stabilize the earth's tectonic plates to ensure we will not have
any overly-drastic planetary cataclysms during these times,
something which has happened in the past when the Earth entered
the part of the solar system it's now moving into.

The Galactic Confederation also sends spiritual energy to us,
helping us to awaken to our soul presence. They specifically assist
the Starseeds – those from other star systems and universes – who
have been incarnating on this planet and know they have a certain
mission to accomplish in the liberation of humanity and the Earth.

Pleiadian Forces Dismantling Nukes

Part of the job of the Galactic Confederation in the last few
decades has been to help prevent planetary disasters as much as
possible. They are watching very closely now as the Cabal panics
and creates destabilizing false flag events in an attempt to start
WW III.

The Pleiadians have been involved in this mission all the way back to the dawn of the nuclear age on Earth, consistently powering down nuclear missiles and melting warheads. The ET ships that have been seen by many around the nuclear missile bases belong to the Pleiadians, as they have a technology to block most of the nuclear weapons.

We're told that in the late '80s and early '90s, all the remaining nuclear missiles in the US and the USSR were completely ruined, thanks to the Pleiadian Sky Crew. Indeed, according to Cobra, it was apparently the final straw that collapsed the Soviet Union and ended the Cold War.

However, the Pleiadians are able to block only about 90% of these weapons, so they've gotten help from the Earth Alliance Ground Crew to infiltrate the nuclear facilities and discover how to physically de-activate the nuclear weapons on site.

A number of insiders are convinced that nuclear war will not be happening again on Earth. Bob Dean, one of Wilcock's insiders, said very simply, "There is not going to be a nuke war, because the ETs are not going to allow it."

Colonel Ross Dedrickson, a Greer insider, has also given testimony about UFOs and nuclear weapons. He explains that the American government at one point tried to detonate a nuclear weapon on the moon, but was prevented from doing so:

> "I also learned about incidents involving nuclear weapons, and among these incidents were those involving a couple of nuclear weapons sent into space that were destroyed by the extraterrestrials. . . . At the very end of the '70s and the early '80s, we attempted to put a nuclear weapon on the moon and explode it for scientific measurements and other things, which was not acceptable to the extraterrestrials. They destroyed the weapon before it got to the moon."

This information about ETs and nukes even hit the mainstream news when Astronaut Edgar Mitchell publicly claimed: "My own experience has made it clear that the ETs have been attempting to keep us from going to war and are helping to create peace on earth."

Another job the Light Forces have taken on is eliminating depleted uranium -- a lethal substance -- in our skies which the

Cabal has been spraying out there through chemtrails. The Light Forces have also mitigated the damage done in disasters such as the Gulf of Mexico oil spill.

Sphere Being Alliance

A sub-group within the Galactic Forces is the "Sphere Being Alliance", comprised of beings mentioned in Chapter 9, known as the "Blue Avians". Corey Goode tells us they are here to help humanity evolve out of the 3D-4D frequency. They have created an "energetic blockade" around both the Earth and our entire solar system.

They have also come to give us a message:

> "Focus on increasing your service to others and be more loving to yourself and everyone in order to raise your vibrational and consciousness level. Learn to forgive yourself and others (thus releasing karma). This will change the vibration of the planet, raise the shared consciousness of humanity, and change humankind one person at a time – even if that one person is yourself."

Inner Earth Alliance

The third Light Force Alliance is the "Inner Earth Alliance". This is composed mainly of freedom fighters from many of the star races who have been living within the Earth.

One of the largest components of the Inner Earth Alliance is the "Agarthan Network", made up of the inner-earth Agarthans described in Chapter 10. This network is connected with the Pleiadians and other ET races in the Galactic Confederation and is focused on stabilizing the situation on the planet and giving humanity both physical and spiritual support. They are also ensuring that only the positive timelines for the future of the planet are now possible.

Another inner earth group involved in the Alliance has been described by Corey Goode: the Mayan Group, who are "mandated to be of service to others". He states that back when the Mayans were on Earth, they had originally come from the Pleiades. At one point, their population here grew to over 40 million people.

Then they disappeared from the Earth because their galactic family members came to take them home. But they did leave a contingent behind who have been living in underground bases ever since and are now assisting humanity through the ascension process.

Alliances Working Together – The Resistance Movement

In many ways, the Earth Alliance, the Galactic Alliance, and the Inner Earth Alliance are all working together to free humanity. In essence, they are attempting to "sandwich" the Cabal between the air and the Inner Earth, leaving them no place to run.

An interesting story comes from Cobra about a gathering comprised of all three contingents of the Light Forces Alliance.

In 1975, a certain intelligence agent with the codename "Michael" was running for his life from the Cabal. He gathered around him a group of twelve operatives in order to protect himself. While on the run and in hiding, they discovered a maze of tunnels below the New York underground subway system. They entered these tunnels, disappeared from the surface, and then formed what became known as the "Organization". Their objective was to overthrow the rule of the Illuminati and give advanced technologies to humanity. Their main command center was under the subway system of New York.

Living underground, the Organization eventually came in contact with the civilization of Agartha which had been there for several millennia. Those beings put them in contact with the Andromedans they were working with. Together this group all went on a mission to overthrow the Dark Forces in other places in the solar system. When they arrived back on Earth, they united and emerged as one group known as the "Resistance Movement".

In the late 1990s, with the assistance of the Pleiadians and other Galactic Confederation forces, the Resistance Movement group helped to clear out most of the remaining Reptilian forces in the solar system.

According to Cobra, this sent the Cabal into panic mode, which gave birth to 9/11 – an attempt to preserve their last stronghold on the planet. As horrific as 9/11 was, it did not turn out as the Cabal had planned. It served instead as an awakening for much of humanity as to what has been going on behind the scenes for a very long time.

This new awareness has made it easier for the Resistance Movement to move more deeply into their strategies to overthrow the Cabal. By 2003, they had cleared all the deep Cabal underground military bases, and only the uppermost portions of those bases remained. In addition, all remaining underground storages of gold, precious objects and artifacts were removed from the Cabal's control.

Another optimistic report from multiple sources is that at this point all negative timelines have now been erased. There is no possibility for global destructive plans of the Cabal to come to fruition, no WWIII, no New World Order, no mass depopulation, no FEMA camps.

What remains to be dealt with, along with a number of the Chimera Group Cabal members still functioning, are the Cabal's threats of detonating "toplet" bombs. Evidently, when these weapons are put under extreme pressure and temperature, it causes a reaction that could actually annihilate the entire planet. That is why the Alliances are being so careful and taking all the time they need to make their moves.

Cobra does indicate that something intense may occur right before the "Event" (described in Chapter 16) which will signal the beginning of collective ascension on the planet. And that is a military confrontation between the Light Forces and the segment of the Air Force that is still under the control of the Cabal. It if does occur, he assures us it will be a brief battle and that the Light Forces will be victorious.

The Light Alliances will be working behind the scenes until a certain degree of awareness on the planet is reached. At that point, most likely not long before the first contact with the positive ETs happens, they will also make themselves known to the surface populations.

Many within the Light Force Alliances are now insisting that disclosure happen and soon. As we've seen, the Cabal is attempting to control and stage-manage disclosure as much as possible, wanting only partial disclosure. But many sources are now saying this will not be possible for them.

We Have our Own Part to Play

As wonderful as it is to know that we have all this help from the Light Alliances assisting us to clean up the mess on our planet, it's important to understand that the ETs will not just sweep in to rescue us, as some people tend to believe. The ETs have made this clear. We have to do our part in this process as well as we are able, as this is essential to our learning and evolution.

However, they will guide and protect us along the way. They will help mitigate the damage still being perpetrated by the Cabal and any dark ET forces that are left in our atmosphere.

Light Force Alliances – References

Earth Alliance
1. Cobra. "Prosperity Packages and 6000 Inventions."
http://prepareforchange.net/what-is-the-resistance-movement/
2. Salla, Michael. "World Religions Unite as Prelude to Extraterrestrial Disclosure".
http://exopolitics.org/world-religions-unite-as-prelude-to-extraterrestrial-disclosure/
3. Wilcock, David. "Downfall of the Cabal".
https://www.youtube.com/watch?v=IWHyrvFODb8&feature=youtu.be

Inner Earth Alliance
1. Cobra. "The Resistance." http://prepareforchange.net/what-is-the-resistance-movement/
2. Glade, Danell. "What is the Resistance Movement?"
http://prepareforchange.net/what-is-the-resistance-movement/
3. Goode, Corey. "ETs and Inner Earth Beings".
https://spherebeingalliance.com/blog/transcript-ets-and-inner-earth-beings.html

Galactic Alliance
1. Beckow, Steve. "Introduction to...What's Happening in our World".
http://goldenageofgaia.com/2017/06/30/an-introduction-to-whats-happening-in-our-world/
2. Coloborama. "Return to Light – Cobra".
http://2012portal.blogspot.pt/2017/07/return-to-light.html
3. Davidson, Gordon Asher. *The Transfiguration of our World*.
https://www.amazon.com/Transfiguration-Our-World-Alliance-Transforming/dp/0983569134/ref=sr_1_1?s=books&ie=UTF8&qid=1507706651&sr=1-1&keywords=Gordon+Asher+Davidson
4. Gabriel, Elora *and* Kirschbaum, Karen. *"The Return of Light"*.
http://www.thenewearth.org/returnoflight.html
5. Walia, Arjun. "The United States Tried To Detonate A Nuclear Weapon On The Moon & Somebody Responded When We Did".
http://prepareforchange.net/next-story-united-states-tried-detonate-nuclear-weapon-moon-somebody-responded/

All Alliances
1. Arr, Diane. "The Event and the Resistance".
http://prepareforchange.net/transcript-coast-coast-cobra-january-2013/
2. As You Wish Radio Show with James Gilliland and Sierra Neblina.
https://bbsradio.com/podcast/you-wish-talk-radio-august-12-2017
3. Carty, Jonathan. "Voice Guided Video to The Event"
http://prepareforchange.net/voice-guided-video-event-432-hz/

4. Cobra. "Resistance Movement".
http://2012portal.blogspot.com/2012/04/resistance-movement-normal-0.html#comment-form

Chapter 14

Human Lightworker Alliance

There is a fourth group within the Light Force Alliance, whether members within it are aware of it or not. And that is the ever-expanding group of human Lightworkers who are waking up to the fact they have a mission to accomplish during these times. Indeed, Cobra tells us the Galactic Alliance uses the energy emanating from Lightworkers as a battery source in order to most effectively do their work.

If you know yourself to be a Lightworker, it's important to understand this. What you do in your daily life, what you think, what you feel, and how high you keep your vibration are all significant in contributing to the collective consciousness of the Light Alliances.

The more you focus on Light, the more this adds to the collective battery of Light. The more compassion you have for yourself and others, the more you strengthen this love energy within the Light Forces. Be careful about doubting the impact your consciousness has on the effectiveness of the Light Forces. It is more powerful than you know.

Indeed, Cobra maintains that Lightworker activity is essential for liberation (or the "Event") to even happen. He says that a major factor holding it back is

> "...the deep mind-programmed state of the surface humanity which has chosen the slowest path possible towards the Event. Now a small minority of people is over-performing and carrying the load of Liberation for many, whereas the vast majority is under-performing and just complaining."

He adds:

> "Many people are asking me what to do to speed up the Event. The answer is very simple: each of you has been born with a mission. Go inside, discover that mission and carry it out. All our missions combined will create the Event."

Dealing with Discouragement and Disillusionment

It is understandable that you may fall at times into periods of discouragement and disillusionment when you feel you've failed to accomplish what you've hoped to as a Lightworker. Or when your third-dimensional patterns arise and pull you into self-doubt and depression. These feelings are fairly common among Lightworkers.

It can be helpful to know that as a member of this human Lightworker group, you may have taken the fullest brunt of the Darkness that has corrupted this planet. For not only have you fallen victim to the controlling nature of the Darkness throughout all the ages you've been attempting to bring the Light into the Dark – you have also seen that Darkness is not the true nature of humanity, and the suffering you've witnessed may break your heart.

Also, as a Lightworker, you may also be a starseed, someone who came to Earth from somewhere out in the universe to assist humanity. And if so, you may remember your original Light-filled galactic home in the stars that others have no memories of, and this might often bring on a sense of homesickness and loneliness.

In addition, you may experience stirrings of memory of all the times you've lost faith in past lives when not enough help arrived to assist you with the "rescue mission" you were on. You've likely lived through times of feeling totally abandoned and betrayed and have wanted to simply give up.

Primary Implant

Cobra offers help in understanding a basic truth about our condition as starseed Lightworkers. He tells us that upon entrance into the quarantined Earth for many thousands of years, all Souls have been required to receive an implant he calls the "Primary

Implant". This implant is in place in every human being, positioned in the frontal lobe of the brain "on the plasma and etheric planes".

Very importantly, this implant holds the primary message that we are *separate from the Source/Love/Light*. This sense of disconnection serves to attract situations that reflect that disconnection and create even more suffering. When our free will aligns with the implant's message, the Light Forces tend to have difficulty intervening in our life, our prayers have a harder time being answered, our protection is lessened, and our trust can be severed.

Cobra explains that these implants were created by the Chimera Group millions of years ago and were reinforced in humanity when they brought about what he calls the "Great Forgetting of 1996" in order to prevent planetary ascension.

The good news is that the key to resolve this situation is primarily for us to be aware of the existence of this implant. Mere awareness of it and the mind program associated with it will accelerate its dissolution.

When we stay aware of this implant, the Light Forces are able to intervene in our lives more directly, and our requests and prayers are more easily answered. Cobra also tells us that when a critical mass of these implants is dissolved, the whole reality construct of duality, Darkness, and suffering will collapse – and the Light will be able to return to all.

Dealing with Guilt, Shame & Self-Doubt

Something else to be aware of as a Lightworker is that part of the "Archonic programming" we've all received is that we are to blame for our suffering. Old religious teachings, from both the East and the West, have been corrupted by the Dark throughout the eons, in essence telling us that we are responsible for our pain. They assert that we are sinful, we are inherently flawed, we need to fix ourselves, and we have to forgive ourselves for evil actions of the past. In essence, the message – whether overt or implied – is that we are inherently flawed beings needing to redeem ourselves.

Even more "enlightened" New Age teachings have threads of this message in them. They often tell us that we're still here working out "bad" karma because we need to "pay for" all the negative actions we've taken in the past. We can't become enlightened because we're not "ready" yet, we're not healed enough, we're not "spiritual" enough. With this message in the mix, it's no wonder so many Lightworkers are constantly working with issues of guilt, shame and self-doubt.

God's "Lessons" and "Tests"

Another type of distortion stemming from certain religious and even some of the New Age teachings is that there are "tests" and "lessons" from God we need to endure and hopefully pass. The distortion is the assertion that these tests and lessons come from God, when in truth they are simply the result of living on a fallen planet. Many of the trials and tribulations in our history have nothing to do with our evolution or our awakening process; they only exist because we are imprisoned in this darkened planet.

This can be difficult to understand, because the distortions have all been interwoven very cleverly into the Truth. Some of what spiritual teachings assert is true; some of it is not. In one way, we *are* responsible for working through the karma we've created. And it's true we are not experiencing full awakening because we are not yet ready for it.

What is usually missing, however, is the understanding that the karmic wheel and the reincarnation system were hijacked by the Dark when they arrived here, skewing them in such a way as to make it next to impossible to ever free ourselves from the karmic wheel. And that the invading forces brought with them a Darkness that pervades just about everything we experience here. We also don't learn that these beings inserted implants into our consciousness that make it very difficult to feel our connection to Source.

We are inherently Beings of pure Light and Love. That is our true essence. We simply volunteered for a task of dealing with Darkness which required that our Essence be corrupted by it, and thus have all but forgotten who we really are.

If anything, if there is such a thing as a "test", it has been about our commitment and adherence to the principles of Light. And this we have obviously passed, if we are still here and are focusing on being a Lightworker. It is actually miraculous that we have held onto the Light at all, considering what we have endured. It is a miracle to rejoice about.

Taking Responsibility without Assuming Guilt

In realizing this, we can drop any attitude when working on ourselves that promotes a feeling of guilt, shame or low self-worth, which just compounds the work we already need to do. It is true that we need to work through the karma we have created, but it need not be done with the faulty belief that because we have it, there's something wrong with us.

The work of releasing our karma needs to be done instead with a knowing that in coming here to assist humanity, we willingly took on the responsibility of experiencing all that was here to experience – all the Darkness, all the suffering due to the distorted karmic system, and all the consequences that would occur from this choice. It was part of the contract we made in incarnating here to accomplish our work.

We can therefore do our healing work with a sense of self-love and self-appreciation. We can recognize how powerful we are to have come here with the mission we did, and to still be fulfilling that mission despite everything we've endured to clear the distortions and the corruptions of the Light that have been created in this world of third-dimensional Earth.

With this attitude, we can then more easily release the old patterns of suffering and limitation we carry. We can essentially shrug them off, like old ill-fitting clothing, rather than feeling we have to suffer our way through a healing process which often brings up emotions of guilt and shame.

Believing only Love and Light are Real

Yet another distortion some Lightworkers grapple with when following certain spiritual teachings is the idea that only the positive is real – only Love and Light actually exist, and all pain and suffering are illusion. And if you experience fear or judgment or any other negative emotion, you simply aren't seeing the "Truth". You aren't awake enough. There's something spiritually deficient about you if you fall into suffering.

Not only does the belief that only Good exists cause a great deal of grief when negativity is experienced, it also prevents seeing what is actually true in the greater reality: that Darkness *does* exist. And we're all subject to its insidious effect on us, especially when under the many stresses this level of reality we're still living in poses.

Again, there is some truth to these ideas about Love and Light. In our original blueprint design, there *is* only Light and Love – this is our true Essence. And it's definitely important to remember this. However, to insist that Darkness is only illusion just creates the desired effect the Dark Forces intend – that we experience low self-esteem and self-judgment when we can't sustain a positive state of Love and Light.

Activating Your Mission

Many Lightworkers are feeling an urgency at this point to be doing their Soul Mission and are feeling frustrated. Either they don't know what their mission is – only that they have one – or they can't seem to get started on it. Something seems to constantly block its manifestation.

If you find yourself in this place, know that a lot of things have to be in place first before certain spiritual missions can get started, including the Earth and humanity being in a position to receive what you have to offer. Although it may be true you're not quite "ready" to offer what you've come to give, that more clearing needs to be done to prepare you, it may also be true that everything is not in place yet for your mission to unfold.

Also, others who are to be involved in your mission may not be ready yet. So consider these factors if you believe you're not ready or healed enough to do what you've come to do. Other circumstances may also be playing a part.

Then again, although you believe you probably have a mission, you may not feel called to do anything at all at this point. There might not be anything you feel passionate about. Maybe you feel empty, flat and without interest or motivation to reach out and do anything. If so, let that too be okay. You may simply be in a period of Ascension Clean-Out, a phase of the Void in which past interests and passions are being emptied out, along with any ego agendas you may have attached to them.

This can be an uncomfortable phase of the ascension process, but it's a necessary one. Relax and accept the emptiness you're experiencing, and you will see that there is great peace and relief in doing this.

At some point, passion will likely arise again, because you are here with a mission, one you've likely had for eons of time. And you'll see that this time you will finally be able to accomplish it.

Remembering Your Commitment

James Gilliland speaks in no uncertain terms about the commitment we lightworkers made in coming here during these times:

> "Just remember you bought this E ticket, and Gods and Goddesses don't do boring things. You will be called upon to do your part. There will be many initiations, awakenings, people in all walks of life remembering another way, a better way of living in harmony with each other and nature.
>
> "These are the days of personal responsibility, accountability, and releasing the past. Love is the ultimate power in the universe and love heals. Resistance to love can however be quite uncomfortable."

He states further that past life memories will open up for us – lives in other planes and dimensions, and in advanced civilizations in other star systems. And that these memories are being brought forward, because it is time to "awaken, remember and act".

> "You did not come to be absorbed by a very wounded sick society. You came to change it. You are not alone and there will be a grand reunion. The Star Nations, some returning, many of which have always been here, are a part of this process. They are the greater family of man."

Calling in Protection

If you are someone who is already in the process of activating your mission and embarking on external action, do remember to protect yourself. It's very important, especially as you go out in public, to invoke as much help as you can from the invisible realms, in the form of Archangels, Ascended Masters, Christ Consciousness, ETs – whatever works for you.

Calling in help is necessary for protection whether you're in the process of expressing your soul mission yet or not. All Lightworkers really need to be doing this at this point, as the Dark is currently being flushed out from all beings, from within the earth, and from every dimension, impacting us in a myriad of ways.

Also, as previously noted, keeping yourself surrounded with Divine Light is important to remember, especially if you are with others who are expressing negatively or if you're in large groups of people. Many at this point are in the process of releasing negative energies that are emerging from the unconscious; and as the empath you likely are, you are susceptible to absorbing these energies.

Cutting Cords

Another thing to be aware of are energetic "cords" that you probably have formed with other people in your life, especially with family members and friends (or clients if you're in a healing profession). The cords can drain you of energy and life force. The people you're connected to likely have no desire to drain you, but it's just what occurs when cords are formed with them.

Cutting these cords can be a good practice to include in your daily meditations. They are usually connected to the first three chakras. You may find there are even cords connecting you to ex-lovers or partners which continue to drain you and help prevent you from moving forward in your life.

It's a simple practice: simply tune in the best you can to your lower chakras and ask to become aware of any cords there. When you sense them, simply visualize cutting them or ask that they be cut. If you're not sure of what you're sensing, ask that any that are present be cut. You will feel a release and a balancing of your energy in doing this.

ETs and Light Beings Don't Totally Get It

Because we tend to consider the benevolent ETs, the Archangels and all other Celestial Beings as so much more evolved than we are, we may believe they are all-knowing and all-understanding of our situation here on Earth. Although they do know a great deal more than we do, have powers we don't have, and have spiritual understanding we don't, it is also true that they sometimes really don't get what life here on Earth is like for those of us living in physical bodies.

Often they have never embodied in form in a dimension any lower than the sixth or seventh. And at times they cannot even see clearly what any of us is individually experiencing. They only have a general energetic sense of it, which they are sometimes unable to interpret clearly without the needed reference points of this dimension we're living in.

For this reason, it is important for us to speak clearly with them, giving details about what our experience is like here, dealing with the Darkness in all the ways we are. We need to tell our guides and all others working with us exactly what we need. It's important to be specific and not assume they can always figure things out without our help.

When we're concerned about large groups of the population or events that are affecting certain parts of the world, it's helpful for us to describe to them what we see may be needed. It's as though the Higher Forces now entering into the Earth's field need for us to create a detailed rescue map for them. The more the Light Forces know about the situation here, the better prepared they can be to assist us.

An interesting invitation recently came out on the *Prepare for Change* website, one of the sites on which Cobra's information is posted. They have opened up a communication channel between the ETs in the Resistance Movement and those of us in the "surface population". It's an opportunity for Lightworkers to speak directly to those ETs in the Light Forces, describing our experiences here on Earth and what our concerns and needs are.

Cobra describes the difficulty ETs often have in truly understanding our situation:

> "It is sometimes not simple for them to understand the reactions of the surface population because they are simply...psychologically quite different. And if you explain to them a little bit more, even telepathically or in writing – you can even post an article on your blog and address it to them – that would be a great idea."

Cobra has said that the Resistance has read all the comments people have posted so far and "they are now realizing that the amount of suffering of the surface population is even greater than they imagined".

Ways to Increase our Assistance to the Light Forces

With greater understanding now, the Resistance has suggestions that can help us create positive energy to assist us in our ascension process. This energy we create will also be helpful for them in their tasks. They suggest that in order to decrease suffering, we need to create "positive moments" every day.

Simple methods to do that might include 1) spending time in nature, 2) focusing on something beautiful and inspiring, 3) pursuing a hobby, 4) decreasing our exposure to electronic media, 5) listening to music, and 6) spending quality time with other people.

David Wilcock also reminds us that one important way to assist is to not "feed the Cabal" with what is known to insiders as "loosh" – an energetic substance the Cabal feeds on, comprised of negative emotions such as fear, shame, anger and depression.

In fact, one of our greatest weapons is to spend a lot of time laughing, which creates a very high vibration. He postulates that if the majority of people on the Earth were to laugh for just one day, the Cabal would be defeated.

Mass Meditations

Also, as noted earlier, joining in group meditations that are offered, both online and in person, is another way to greatly increase the light on the planet. These meditations help to create a "Unified Light Grid", thus making it easier for the Light Forces to make headway in defeating the Darkness. This Grid is reportedly growing stronger day by day.

Indeed, in a mass meditation called by Cobra and others for the August 21, 2017 eclipse, more than a quarter million people are said to have participated. The meditation was designed to create energy for the Light Forces in their final endeavors to defeat the Dark Forces.

It was also designed to help ready humanity for the upcoming "Event" Cobra has referred to for a number of years, a tremend-ously powerful global event that will be the beginning of humanity's collective ascension. (See Chapter 16 for details.)

After the meditation, Cobra reported:

"The unity and the resonance we have achieved was remarkable and was a signal ... that the awakened part of the human population will be able to hold the Light in unity when the Event happens and that it is now time to put this planet through the Ascension process. This means that from now on, the energies from the Galactic Center will exponentially intensify until all darkness is purified and the planet is liberated."

He further stated that during the meditation, the critical mass of the "New Atlantis energy grid" around the planet had been completed and that this grid was now strong enough to handle the energies of the Event. From now on, the New Atlantis energy grid would be used by the Light Forces to "transmit mission activation codes in the form of revelatory dreams, impressions and visions to the awakened part of the human population".

The Final Battle

So, as of September 2017, this is what is happening on Earth in the final battle in this universe between the Dark and Light Forces. All the rest of the Universe has already been liberated, and this is the last stronghold of the Dark. We are currently in the phase that has often been described as the "darkness that occurs right before dawn".

It is no accident that we are all here at this time – to witness and experience this monumental event and finally complete our spiritual missions by being part of it.

As we move through this process of planetary liberation, and this last planet in our universe is set free, it is said this will be a fulfillment of an ancient galactic prophecy that there would come a time when the galactic network of Light would be completed and Darkness would no longer exist.

Human Light Worker Alliance - References

1. Cobra - The Portal Blog 8-23-17.
http://2012portal.blogspot.com/2017/08/unity-meditation-report.html
2. Coloborama. Prepare for Change. http://prepareforchange.net/blog/
3. Gabriel, Elora *and* Kirschbaum, Karen. *"The Return of Light"*.
http://www.thenewearth.org/returnoflight.html
4. Gilliland, James. "We're in for a Wild Ride".
http://goldenageofgaia.com/2017/08/09/james-gilliland-were-in-for-a-wild-ride/
5. The Earth Plan website. "The Return of Light ~ Revelations from the Creator God Horus ~ Elora Gabriel and Karen Kirschbaum"
http://theearthplan.blogspot.com/2014/05/the-return-of-light-revelations-from.html
6. Wilcock, David. *Ascension Mysteries*, pg. 432 ("Loosh").
https://www.amazon.com/Ascension-Mysteries-Revealing-Cosmic-Between-ebook/dp/B0191ZL2EC

Chapter 15

Downfall of the Cabal

So the final battle between the cosmic Dark and Light Forces is underway and the outcome looks hopeful. But there is one important aspect of this battle, we're told, that is mainly up to the Earth Alliance – and that's bringing down the Cabal. This is not an easy task. They exist in numerous governments and institutions across the planet, and the ones who are the most powerful are often the most hidden.

Indeed, there are those in the thick of this war who claim there is still a great deal the "White Hats" have yet to accomplish to rid the planet of the Cabal's control, especially in America. Some are saying we are on a trajectory that could fork in one of two ways: to a calm and systematic dismantling of the Dark – or to civil war within America.

Simon Parkes, a powerful British psychic who speaks out clearly about what he sees for humanity, has cautioned that the war is not over and some major challenges lie ahead. He warns that we shouldn't drop our guard. Internet data mining expert Clif High, another crusader in this war, says his "internet spiders" indicate that a financial crash of some kind is imminent.

Encouraging Progress

Nonetheless, those like David Wilcock, Corey Goode, James Gilliland, Gordon Asher Davidson, and Cobra, who perhaps have access to what's happening on a more cosmic level, have proclaimed that tremendously encouraging progress has been made toward liberating the planet.

A great many others are also doing their utmost to bring awareness toward forcing the Cabal to their knees. Most of these people have internet sites featuring blogs on disclosure, and/or they give interviews that are posted on video sites.

Aside from those I've mentioned so far in this book, there are other dedicated players who appear on alternative news sites, such as Robert David Steele, Steve Pieczenic, Ben Fulford, Jordan Sather, David Icke, Neil Keenan, and Alex Jones. These people give updates on a wide range of themes, but generally cover subjects having to do with disclosure. They report what is happening behind the scenes in the political arena and new revelations and events regarding the efforts happening globally to bring the Cabal down.

The Cabal is Panicking

An interesting phenomenon to watch is that as the dark ET forces continue to be defeated, the Cabal have become increasingly panicked with the decrease in their ET leadership. Among other things, they're creating more and more false flag events and manipulating weather disasters in an attempt to strengthen their hold on us by creating fear likely to immobilize us.

But people are increasingly seeing through these attempts, recognizing that it's the Cabal that is instigating the attacks. Their whole game is falling apart. In presentations at the "Contact in the Desert" conference in late June of 2017, David Wilcock, James Gilliland, and Corey Goode described at length the events chronicling the downfall of the Cabal.

Neil Keenan, veteran journalist and whistle-blower also tells us that there is no question the Cabal is "on the ropes", although they are still attempting to work their way out of their current predicament:

> "They have their people continually moving surreptitiously with desperate hopes of find-ing ways out of the very swamps they so cleverly (or so they thought) created for themselves...It is our job to finish them off once and for all! No second chances, as there have already been too many chances."

Ben Fulford, another crusader against the Cabal, agrees they are losing control at last. He has focused on keeping tabs on what is happening with the "Khazarian Mafia" – a powerful arm of the Cabal that has ruled the West for thousands of years:

> "The Khazarian Mafia, still unable to comprehend their ongoing historic defeat, are fanatically trying yet again to start World War 3, multiple sources agree. However, the balance of world power has now tipped decisively against them."

In speaking of the Cabal, visionary James Gilliland states:

> "We are at the turning point, their contract is up, time and a half is over and they are being removed along with their unseen puppet masters. The Sun is cooperating with the Earth's desire to ascend. It is as if the whole multiverse is behind this event."

He further states:

> "The awakening and healing process is in full swing. We are witnessing the end of tyranny and the beginning of a whole new age. It is the prophecies unfolding. The draconian grid or archon grid, as some call it, is collapsing. A new 5D grid is pressing in to take its place. It is what the Mayans refer to as the 9th wave or unity consciousness. Everything that is not frequency specific to these new energies will either transform or fall away."

Disclosure about ETs

Although there is a great amount of disclosure about the secret space programs and ET contact on a number of internet sites, the mainstream media is still holding back from reporting any of the news in this exciting arena.

However, some soft disclosure does seem to be leaking through the MSM. For example, it was reported that the Pope's chief astronomer stated that "life on Mars cannot be ruled out." Writing in the Vatican newspaper, with the headline "Aliens are My Brothers", the astronomer Father Gabriel Funes said intelligent beings created by God could exist in outer space. The search for forms of extraterrestrial life, he says, does not contradict belief in God.

This is especially interesting considering the long dark history of the Church's involvement with the Illuminati. Although there exist varying reports and opinions about Pope Francis's possible involvement with the Illuminati, some sources claim he does seem to be gradually cleaning house and may even be in contact with certain benevolent ETs.

Another possible indication of the Pope's intentions is a press release issued in June 2017, entitled "Churches Unite around ET Disclosure". It tells us that leaders from a diverse collection of religious communities issued a statement for world unity in a video message. The video shows that a group of world religious leaders came together to make a joint statement calling for people to embrace friendship and unity and to overcome division.

This joint statement is an important message in its own right. But what lends the message added significance is recent information from Corey Goode that a group of positive extraterrestrials is working with religious leaders in promoting world unity and disclosure.

He claims that the call to world unity is a "prelude to disclosure of extraterrestrial life". In fact, he says that several different groups of ETs are now committed to open contact with humanity, and they've started the process by contacting world religious leaders to act as intermediaries in this process.

Pedophile Arrests

The area of disclosure that might be the most gratifying to many at this point is that of the arrests taking place in a number of Cabal-related human trafficking rings – and, in particular, pedophile rings that exist across the planet. As of June 2017, there had been hundreds of recent arrests in the US, Europe and other countries. Journalist Jonathan Carty cited a long list of these arrests in his post "Pedo Arrests and Disclosures Continue".

According to a report soon afterward on an international website, PressTV, a huge global pedophile network on the dark web was shut down, resulting in thousands arrested, including "high-level politicians, entertainers, white collar professionals and high-ranking clergy members". German prosecutors said they had shut down a major platform used by "elite pedophiles" for organizing the sexual abuse of children, which led to the arrest of its suspected ringleader and senior members of the pedophile community in Germany and abroad.

Dubbed *Operation Elysium*, the sting was launched on the eve of the G20 in Hamburg, throwing the global summit into disarray after key members of at least two European delegations were held by police.

Further arrests were made globally following the initial raid, in a joint effort involving international law enforcement agencies. In all, there were over 87,000 members discovered to be trading images and videos of "the most serious sexual abuse of children, including babies, and representations of sexual violence against children".

That bust came just two months after nearly 900 members of a global dark web pedophile ring spanning Europe and the Americas were arrested following a two-year investigation by the FBI and Europol.

And yet, surprisingly, these arrests of nearly 88,000 individuals are not even the largest busts in history. Earlier in 2017, another online dark net pedophile platform called *Playpen* had been dismantled. This was a child pornography network that had had 150,000 active pedophiles using the site.

According to David Wilcock, these continuing pedophile arrests will likely be what essentially takes the Cabal down.

Indeed, disclosure about pedophilia is finally hitting the mainstream media big-time at long last. In late October 2017, the New York Times came out with an expose of one of the biggest sex scandals in Hollywood, starring Harvey Weinstein. This has encouraged many actresses and others in Hollywood to speak about their own sexual abuse experiences--especially when they were children in the entertainment industry. Many connections are now being made through these revelations between the Hollywood and the Washington DC Cabal members involved in these scandals.

Arrests Still Pending

Although relatively "small fish" have thus far been arrested for human trafficking and pedophilia, it is definitely a start. From what a number of sources say, they are "saving the big fish" for last.

Some of the arrests have included more than just child porn and sex trafficking. Law enforcement forces have actually infiltrated the

Illuminati's networks in which the dark rituals of child sacrifice have occurred for many centuries. However, this aspect of the Illuminati faction has yet to be significantly uncovered.

We are told that plans to arrest the "big fish" will happen sometime soon when the timing is deemed right. Investigator Ben Fulford tells us that the White Hats are attempting to make the transition very carefully. If the old structures were to collapse too quickly with nothing to replace them, it would create too much chaos, hardship and bloodshed.

As it is, the Cabal, knowing their days are numbered, are already attempting to bring about as much mayhem and destruction as possible before their final defeat, by creating false flag terror events and severe weather conditions. A number of credible sources have reported on the obvious engineering involved in the devastating floods in Texas and Louisiana and the extreme heat and resultant fires in the US northwest in September 2017.

However, increasingly, we are nearing the time when the arrests will finally take place and a stop to all of this destruction will occur. Some say that when this does happen, there may be an approximately two-week power outage as the Alliance goes through the final stages of arresting key Cabal operatives. This is primarily intended to prevent them from fleeing and to minimize panic and civilian casualties during the arrest process.

There are also many other arrests of the Cabal that are in store for crimes other than pedophilia. Several investigators have written about these arrests since 2011, based on insider reports at that time. Two others who speak at length about them are James Gilliland and Sierra Neblina, an investigator and former secret space program abductee.

These two tell fascinating stories about their conscious night travels in which they assist the ETS, Angelics and Ascended Masters in resisting the Dark Forces. They say that initially the Light Forces hoped that the Cabal and dark ETs could be convinced to switch from their dark agendas through a process called "containment", in which an individual would be wrapped in a container of love-infused Light and gently encouraged by Light Beings to switch their agenda to supporting a positive agenda for humanity.

They say this approach worked with some of them, but many refused to turn even after guaranteeing they would. So now no more chances are being given to the Dark Forces to turn toward the Light. These recalcitrant beings are simply being hunted down and either arrested or "sent back to the Central Sun for resetting", whatever that might mean.

However or whenever this process may be complete is not certain. But it does seem that the Light Forces are having considerable success. Without the negative ET leadership the Cabal has always relied on for direction and support, their control is greatly waning. Although we may still be in for some rough and confusing times, the good guys are at last winning the battle.

Downfall of the Cabal - References

David Wilcock
1. Wilcock, David. "Endgame I". http://divinecosmos.com/start-here/davids-blog/1208-endgame-pt-1
2. Wilcock, David. "Downfall of the Cabal". https://www.youtube.com/watch?v=IWHyrvFODb8&feature=youtu.be

Cobra
1. Cobra. "The Event and The Resistance" http://prepareforchange.net/transcript-coast-coast-cobra-january-2013/
2. DaNell, www.prepareforchange.net author. http://prepareforchange.net/dark-forces-hierarchy-control-tactics/

Neil Keenan
1. Keenan, Neil. "The Dismantling of the Cabal". http://neilkeenan.com/neil-keenan-update-the-dismantling-of-the-cabal/
2. Starship Earth: the Big Picture. "Latest Intel from Thomas Williams" http://www.starshipearththebigpicture.com/tag/neil-keenan/

Ben Fulford
1. Fulford, Benjamin Fulford "Khazarian mafia will make several more tries to start WW3 before their final defeat" http://www.stillnessinthestorm.com/2017/06/benjamin-fulford-june-12th-2017-khazarian-mafia-will-make-several-more-tries-to-start-ww3-before-their-final-defeat.html?utm_source=feedburner&utm_medium=email&utm_campaign=Feed%3A+StillnessInTheStormBlog+%28Stillness+in+the+Storm+Blog%29
2. Fulford, Ben. https://geopolitics.co/vital-issues/ben-fulford/q.html?utm_source=feedburner&utm_medium=email&utm_campaign=Feed%3A+StillnessInTheStormBlog+%28Stillness+in+the+Storm%29
3. Fulford, Ben. "August 29th, 2017: Q&A with Benjamin Fulford & a Reader". http://www.stillnessinthestorm.com/2017/08/benjamin-fulford-august-29th-2017-

David Icke
Icke, David. "The End is Near". https://www.youtube.com/watch?v=IoFrmITvNZ0

James Gilliland
Gilliland, James. "We're in for a Wild Ride". http://goldenageofgaia.com/2017/08/09/james-gilliland-were-in-for-a-wild-ride/

Pedophile Arrests

1. Carty, Jonathan. "Pedo Arrests and Disclosures Continue -- June 20th 2017". http://www.stillnessinthestorm.com/2017/06/pedo-arrests-and-disclosures-continue-june-20th-2017.html?utm_source=feedburner&utm_medium=email&utm_campaign=Feed%3A+StillnessInTheStormBlog+%28Stillness+in+the+Storm+Blog%29

2. Editor. "Germany Dismantles a Huge Child Abuse Ring". http://www.presstv.com/Detail/2017/09/04/534018/Russia-THAAD-missile-US-S-Korea-N-Korea-nuclear-bomb-UNSC

3. Greenberg, Jay. "Catholic Archbishop Blows Whistle". http://www.neonnettles.com/news/2708-catholic-archbishop-blows-whistle-pedophile-priests-names-released-in-list

4. Hasson, Peter. "It's not Just Harvey Weinstein--Entertainment Industry Filled with Accused Sex Offenders". http://www.stillnessinthestorm.com/2017/10/its-not-just-weinstein-entertainment-industry-filled-with-accused-sex-abusers.html#more

Cabal and Religions

1. Salla, Michael. World Religions Unite as Prelude to Extraterrestrial disclosurehttp://exopolitics.org/world-religions-unite-as-prelude-to-extraterrestrial-disclosure/

2. Willey, David. "Vatican says aliens could exist" http://news.bbc.co.uk/2/hi/europe/7399661.stm

Chapter 16

The Event

By now it's abundantly clear that the ascension process is not simply an inner shift we're each making into a higher vibration as individuals. It definitely *is* this, and each of us needs to attend to whatever that might mean on a personal level for us. But ascension also includes a process all of us are going through together as a collective group. And this process, as we've seen, is both vast and multi-layered with gradual events occurring on different dimensions.

And yet some say this process may soon erupt into a single powerful event that will become both the end of a long, long era in human history – and also a new beginning. David Wilcock and author Gordon Asher Davidson have used the term "the Day of Revelation" to describe this event. Cobra has simply called it "the Event", a term that has caught on with a great many people.

Much of what you'll read in this chapter about the Event may sound fantastical to you – too strange and perhaps too good to be true. This is understandable. But, as always, I encourage you to simply take the information in and see if it resonates with you on a level deeper than your mind. Just accepting the possibility of what is being described here about the Event can help prepare you for it, should it indeed occur.

What is the Event?

Both Wilcock and Cobra tell us that the Event will be the sudden beginning of the collective ascension process. It will initially manifest with a "galactic pulse", a solar event that is said to occur every twenty-six thousand years or so. This pulse will release a blindingly bright light arriving directly from the central sun which in the past has triggered a mass ascension (a quantum leap in spiritual evolution) on Earth each time it's occurred.

As an avid scholar of ancient texts, Wilcock claims that this phenomenon is described in the Bible and in Zoroastrian, Hindu, Greek and Roman texts, and that 35 ancient cultures hid the science of this cycle in their mythologies. He adds that there is now scientific data and also insider testimony that support this idea of a solar pulse event.

According to both Wilcock and Cobra, when the galactic pulse happens, it will start a process of transforming matter, energy, consciousness and biological life as we know it. The incoming energies from the pulse will begin to flow through the energy field of all humans as a palpable "wave of love". Everyone will have their own individual experience of healing, release of the past, and inner transformation. But also, there will be a general rise in consciousness of all humanity on the planet.

Directly After the Event

Cobra explains that for the first few hours after the solar event, the Resistance Movement will take over all satellite and communication stations in the world, through which we will be able to receive information about what is occurring. Disclosure about the secret space programs and the crimes of the Cabal will be broadcasted on TV channels.

He further claims that intel packages of disclosure have already been downloaded into the computers of major newspaper agencies around the world. Videos have also been prepared. In addition, messages will appear as pop-ups on countless computers.

Mass Arrests

According to a number of sources, part of what we'll be seeing very soon after the Event is a series of mass arrests of the Cabal, who will be taken into custody and held until trials can take place. Within this group will be members from both political parties in the US Congress. We will be assured that they will be prevented from ever having access to positions of power again. Gordon Davidson adds that, in the meantime, the executive, judicial and military will be in charge, although some Superior Court and other justices will be removed.

Global Currency Reset

Once the mass arrests have been accomplished, another momentous occurrence reportedly will take place – a reset of our global financial system. There is a group known as "the Eastern Alliance" which will put this in place. This group is also referred to as the "Chinese Elders", ancient Chinese families who, through their benevolence and wisdom, have been planning the financial reset for quite a while and have been waiting for right timing to put it in motion.

It is said that the new financial system will include the provisions of an act named GESARA, an acronym for "Global Economic Security & Reformation Act". This act is designed, among other things, to reset the planet and humanity on a foundation of sustainable governance and benefit everyone on the planet through a global currency reset (the GCR). It will put the entire global economy back on the gold standard. When implemented, it will affect all 209 sovereign nations in the world.

Suppressed Technologies Released

As this reset happens, free energy technologies and products will also gradually be released to the public, and everyone will eventually have access to natural, renewable sources of energy. Other important technologies developed in the secret space programs which have been suppressed by the Cabal will also be released.

All this will ensure that the natural abundance of this planet will be distributed to everybody, and our eco-systems will eventually be restored. In time, as the earth recalibrates back to its originally-created frequency, organic food and clean water will be easily available to all.

Included in the new technologies will be those which provide healing on all levels. Humanity will finally have the opportunity for true healing, both physical and psychological. In particular, there will apparently be "healing chambers" that will be available to the general public. We will still go through an aging process but it will be a much easier experience.

Inner Healing Made Easier

Cobra continues to assure us that, with the removal of the Archons from the inner planes, their interference with human relationships will disappear. Many of the old conflicts and dramas which now exist, especially those between men and women, will diminish and unconditional Love will prevail. War will be obsolete.

However, even once the Event has happened, we will all initially still be involved in our individual ascension process, releasing our old third-dimensional habit patterns. Although the Event will give us a collective boost in vibration, reportedly only a small group will make their full ascension into the Fifth Dimension at that time. Most people will continue on with their ascension process.

Nonetheless, it will be a whole lot easier. After the Event, there will be a lot of energy support from the Galactic Central Sun to help us shift into 5D consciousness. The Event will also make it much easier to develop psychic abilities, such as telepathy and clairvoyance. The Light Forces will give guidance and instructions on these tools natural to 5D consciousness.

First Contact

We are told that at some point when enough people on the planet are able to comfortably accept the reality of ETs, Beings within the various galactic civilizations who have assisted us in the liberation process will reveal themselves in an event known as "First Contact". Over time, humanity will eventually be ready to become co-partners in the Galactic Confederation and be able to connect with other sovereign races throughout the galaxy.

Not Everyone will be Ascending

However, as may be obvious as we consider the whole of humanity at this point, not everyone will be making the shift toward 5D consciousness at the time of the Event. The anticipated solar event will require a shift which will prove to be too much for those people who are not ready to ascend at this time. If they haven't already left the planet by the time of the Event, they will leave at the time it occurs or soon thereafter. At death they will be taken to another part of the universe still functioning in the Third Dimension where they can continue their soul evolution.

It's Just the Beginning

Although abrupt in some ways, the Event is not going to be a sudden miraculous shift that changes everything overnight. It is simply the beginning of a gradual process which will eventually result in a much higher consciousness for humanity as a whole and a better physical, psychological and spiritual existence for everybody. In essence, it will be a transition from a 3D-4D world to a 4D-5D one.

At some point, all of humanity will eventually be functioning in 5D consciousness. Although it will take a while for everyone to make this shift, the Event will be the initial boost to get the process in gear and make it a lot easier for us to make the shift.

When Will the Event Happen?

Of course, everyone wants to know when the Event is going to happen. No one speaking about it can give a concrete answer, as so much is still unfolding, and the ever-present factor of free will makes it difficult to predict anything for certain.

Although presenting a somewhat different scenario from that of Cobra for the Day of Revelation, Gordon Asher Davidson concurs with him that all is being very carefully planned and orchestrated by the Light Alliances so that the shift will be universal, seamless and easily accepted by people across the world. He states that the timing will be determined by a large number of factors, including energetic astrological alignments, final preparation and readiness of new systems to be put into place, and the openness and demand of humanity for deep and true transformation in the world.

Also it seems clear that the Event cannot occur until the Light Forces have been absolutely victorious – until all the dark ET-run forces are completely eliminated from our planet. It's also necessary that the grid circling the Earth keeping us in quarantine be completely dismantled.

As we've seen, this is happening fairly rapidly at this point, late 2017. Also, according to Cobra, liberation includes the elimination of the beings known as the Archons existing on the inner planes who have been controlling humanity through their manipulation of the karmic process and the implants and other AI technology they have employed to impede humanity's spiritual evolution.

One of Wilcock's insiders said to him, "The event you expected to happen in 2012 will more likely occur in 2017". Corey Goode states that his intel indicates it will more likely occur sometime between 2018 and 2023.

Even if it takes that long, it is definitely an event worth waiting for. Ascension into the Fifth Dimension is what we are all here for. A few more years will whiz past us, just as the last few years have. And, who knows? The Event could happen tomorrow.

Do you feel prepared for it?

The Event – References

1. Arr, Dane. "The Event". http://prepareforchange.net/transcript-coast-coast-cobra-january-2013/
2. Carty, Jonathan. "Voice Guided Video to The Event"
http://prepareforchange.net/voice-guided-video-event-432-hz/
3. Cobra. "The Event and The Resistance".
 http://prepareforchange.net/transcript-coast-coast-cobra-january-2013/
 4. Cobra. "Interview FAQ: The Event".
http://prepareforchange.net/cobra-interview-faq/#titleArchive
5. Davidson, Gordon Asher. *The Transfiguration of our World*.
https://www.amazon.com/Transfiguration-Our-World-Alliance-Transforming/dp/0983569134/ref=sr_1_1?s=books&ie=UTF8&qid=1507706651&sr=1-1&keywords=Gordon+Asher+Davidson
6. Sumner, Therese Zumi. "The Event Flash – the Galactic Wave of Love".
http://www.theeventchronicle.com/the-event/event-flash-galactic-wave-love/
7. Wilcock, David. *Ascension Mysteries*.
https://www.amazon.com/Ascension-Mysteries-Revealing-Cosmic-Between-ebook/dp/B0191ZL2EC
8. Wilcock, David. "David Wilcock August 21 2017 - UFO Conference | Brand New Disclosure Update".
https://www.youtube.com/watch?v=NNk1lHfyCx8

Chapter 17

Remembering You're a Lightworker

At this writing, it's clear there's a whole lot more going on in the big picture on Earth than meets the eye – to say the least. When you take in all that's been addressed in this book, it can be somewhat overwhelming at first.

And yet, hopefully, you're realizing the importance of being informed – that it's not enough to simply focus on the positive and do your best to act from Love and Light in your daily life. You also need to be aware of the depth and scope of the ways the Dark has played a significant role within all of our lives. It's necessary to be aware of *all* the truth – not just the comfortable aspects of it.

But where does reading all this leave you? Just watching the visible geopolitical battles occurring on the global stage is unnerving and scary enough, let alone knowing now about the battles occurring both out in space and inside the Earth. You may find yourself wanting to leave this world, feeling you can't handle it anymore. You may wish to retreat into your home, hoping to avoid social situations – or resort to drugs and alcohol to drown out the pain and the feeling of helplessness.

Keeping in Mind What You're Here to Do

But if you are a Lightworker, you know this is not the way to go. If you're here to assist humanity and the Earth to make it through the shift to the Fifth Dimension, you know you can't opt out now. This is the time to step forward and live as the Lightworker you know yourself to be.

Actually, as dire as it can seem now, if you tune in you will feel how close we actually are to the finish line, how close we are to being able to live from our true identity as powerful multi-dimensional Beings of Light. We are almost at the finish line.

So instead of getting caught up in all the negativity and chaotic disasters that are currently arising in the world – along with the fear, the anger, the confusion arising from them – you can instead focus on the all the positive that is also occurring. Being able to do this, even while recognizing the Dark control that is still in place, can bring power to you as a Lightworker.

You can rise above fears that arise by realigning to the universal flow of Love/Light energy that is now streaming into the Earth. You likely already know how to embrace the love vibration within you through focusing on gratitude and mindfulness. And you probably know how to listen closely to your intuition. Realize you are equipped with all you will need to make it through this last round of crises within this quickly shifting world.

People Are Waking Up

You can also look around and see that your job as a Lightworker is actually getting easier as time goes on, simply because more and more people are waking up. Indeed you might be surprised to hear that, paradoxically, the world is actually becoming a more peaceful place. A recent research study reported in *The Better Angels of Our Nature: Why Violence has Declined* by Harvard psychologist Steven Pinker reveals that:

> "The news is a systematically misleading way to understand the world. In the past five years alone, conflicts have ended in Chad, Peru, Iran, India, Sri Lanka, India, and Angola; and if peace talks currently underway in Colombia are a success, war will have vanished from the Western hemisphere."

Pinker writes that wars formerly spanned the entire globe. There were 30 of them between 1945 and 1990 that killed 100,000 people or more, including wars in Greece, China, Mozambique, Algeria, Tibet, Guatemala, Uganda, and East Timor.

With the exception of the war occurring in Ukraine at the time of the study in 2015, the zone of war had contracted to a small crescent from central Africa through the Middle East into South Asia. Pinker further states that almost every other kind of violence, including murders, capital punishment, domestic violence, torture and hunting, has also fallen sharply.

Of course, other trouble spots have appeared since the book's release at the end of 2015, but the statistics still remain. Except for skirmishes, there have been no major wars. The Cabal is definitely on its way out. And those that have controlled them are being eliminated. It's important to keep these facts in mind.

The Kids are Already Awake

Another study gives cause for optimism in what seems like a "gloomy present". Mike Males, in his article "The Kids are All Right", tells us that research suggests that young Americans are turning away from crime and drugs and toward tolerance and inclusivity.

> "This isn't "kids are all right!" romanticism; it's a confluence of hard facts and trends. As American politics seems increasingly hopeless, striking generation gaps in attitudes and behaviours have emerged."

He states that the census finds Americans under 25 (51% white, 25% Latino, 14% black, 5% Asian, 5% other/mixed) to be far more diverse than their elders (aged 55+: 74% white). In California, nearly three-quarters of young people now are of color, and half have at least one foreign-born parent. It's clear that this is what America's future looks like.

In focusing on California, Males found that the teenage youth population in that state grew by one million from 1990 to 2015, during an era of increasing poverty and lack of employment. Nonetheless, the Department of Justice, Centers for Disease Control, and census figures show that, among the youth:

➢ Murder arrests fell from 658 to 88 in Los Angeles (and in the crime-ridden city of Compton, from 269 to 8).
➢ Violent crimes: from 21,000 to 7,000.
➢ Property felonies: from 54,000 to 7,000.
➢ Total criminal arrests: from 220,000 to 63,000.
➢ Gun killings: from 351 to 84.
➢ Juvenile imprisonments: from 10,000 to 700
➢ Teenage births from: 26,000 to 7,000.

> ➤ School dropout rates: from 16 per cent to 6 per cent – and college enrolment and graduation soared (from 34 per cent to 47 per cent).

In the 1970s, 10% of young Californians were arrested every year; in the 1990s, 7%; July 2017, 2%. As these figures show, California teenagers are veering away from crime more than adults are in nearly all indexes. And while California's trends are especially pronounced, FBI and CDC data shows major declines in youth problems occurring across the country, as well.

It's interesting to note that these changes have not happened because authorities "got tough"; just the opposite. Very few youths get busted for pot, drinking, curfew or similar offenses anymore; "underage" arrests in all categories are fast disappearing. The credit for improvements appears to lie with the younger generation itself.

Young people are showing signs of being more awake, both socially and politically: polls and surveys consistently show youth in the US strongly support gay marriage (and universally accept interracial marriage), religious tolerance, a "welcome all" stance toward immigrants, scientific reasoning rather than religious faith, action to reverse climate change, proactive government action on the economy and health care, and candidates who act on these agendas.

This is a revolution, a sign of the times to come.

People are Taking Action

Yet another hopeful sign is that, even without knowing the full story about the Cabal or the dark ET forces still controlling us, people of all ages across the globe are pushing past their sense of powerlessness, both individually and as part of collective movements. They are getting around all the manipulation and control of the Cabal, doing what they can to create the New Earth here and now.

You don't have to look far to see this. There are films documenting what certain groups of people have already accomplished in creating the kind of world they want to live in. For example, the film "Tomorrow" released in 2017, the Michael Moore movie "Where to Invade Next", and a film called "Living the Change" all document successful endeavors people have made to greatly improve conditions in their part of the world. There are also a great number of inspiring TED Talks and youtubes by people who are busy manifesting a world we all would wish to live in.

While their numbers are small, these examples are seeding an increasing number of local initiatives to better serve local communities. This is change at the grass roots level – change that can be very successful and powerful in creating the new Earth.

Remembering Who Most of Humanity Is

In addition, it can really help if you consider that "everyday" people – most of us on the planet – are horrified at war, abuse, and violence. Because we see so much violence around us through the news, in movies and on TV, we have become inured to it. But deep within, most of us still abhor it; we are not all violent, murderous barbaric sociopaths.

We have simply been controlled and manipulated by a few who are – and even they have been manipulated by even more powerful dark forces. Most of humanity is not intrinsically violent. Many are spiritually ignorant, caught in fear, and are subject to negative programming they've inherited. Born in an environment of violence, control and limited autonomy, it's all they know.

But the number of these individuals is so much smaller than the rest of us who see life more clearly and live basically ethical lives. It's important to keep a realistic and positive view of humanity in this way, and also to see the power that we as peace-loving humans actually have.

Helping Others to Awaken

As Beings who are awake to our spiritual nature and to the reality of what is happening in the world, perhaps it is our task to turn to those who are not yet awake. We know about the Cabal's agenda, we know about the Light Alliances, we know that humanity can win this epic challenge if people are informed. So we can now start spreading the word to others, telling them about the bigger picture, thus helping to awaken and empower them.

The greater the number of awakened people spreading the word, the faster we as a collective can reach the critical mass of consciously awakened individuals needed to co-create a turn-around for planetary transformation. The hundredth monkey principle will certainly kick in at some point.

It can be helpful to learn how to effectively speak to others about what you know, however. One thing to keep in mind is to share your knowledge in a simple and light way, without a great deal of heaviness or doom and gloom. Stay neutral, strong, and compassionate – and whenever you can, positive. Also be aware when a person's eyes begin to glaze over, indicating they've heard enough for the time-being. With some people, you can only hope to plant seeds for the time-being.

And, of course, one of the best ways to invite people's curiosity is to live your own life in a positive way. If you live with an open heart and have the expectation to see positive improvements happening in the world and in your own life, this can be a very welcoming outlook to others around you. It motivates them to ask questions about what you know and believe to be true.

However you choose to "spread the Light", know that you are part of an increasingly powerful group of Lightworkers in the world. And that you are working in concert with a multitude of ETs here to help liberate the Earth, once and for all. Feel the power and joy in being part of this transformative force on the planet.

The Hero's Journey

The story of humanity's enslavement and liberation can be seen in the context of the classic "Hero's Journey". Joseph Campbell clearly describes this archetypal journey made by heroes in epic stories, legends, and myths.

The hero starts out on a journey to explore the world with great optimism and a sense of adventure. As he travels into the unknown, he is confronted with enormous odds and challenges by the "evil forces" that seem for a while to be insurmountable. Then help of a higher nature comes along to assist him; but it's clear that he must also rise into his highest consciousness and discover his own abilities to assist himself, as well. In the end, he is victorious. He has faced both the inner and outer forces of evil and conquered them. And he is now returning home.

This is humanity's story – a story that is not quite finished. The Dark Forces, both inner and outer, are not yet fully conquered. But victory is near and it is not too early to begin celebrating the triumph of the human spirit.

Nor is to too early to celebrate your own personal triumph as an individual human Lightworker, for you have likely been on your own personal hero's journey for many thousands of years. And you are nearing your own liberation – ascension into the Fifth Dimension.

Despite the darkness that still seems to fill the world, it is already time to dance.

Remembering You're a Lightworker – References

1. Anderson, Julie. "There is More to Life Than This".
http://humansarefree.com/2017/05/there-is-more-to-life-than-this.html
2. Males, Mike. "The Kids are All Right (and these surprising statistics
prove it)". https://www.positive.news/2017/perspective/28490/kids-right-surprising-statistics-prove/
3. Morag. "Earth Warriors, The Frontline, And Trusting Our Instincts"
https://higherdensity.wordpress.com/2017/05/25/morag-in5d-earth-warriors-the-frontline-and-trusting-our-instincts-5-25-17/
4. Phillips, Paul A. "Now That You've Awakened How Do You Awaken
Others?" https://www.newparadigm.ws/my-blogs/now-that-you-ve-awakened-how-do-you-awaken-others/
5. Pinker, Steven. The Better Angels of Our Nature: Why Violence has
Declined. https://www.amazon.com/s/ref=nb_sb_noss?url=search-alias%3Dstripbooks&field-keywords=The+Better+Angels+of+Our+Nature%3A+Why+Violence+has+Declined
6. Wilcock, David. Ascension Mysteries.
https://www.amazon.com/Ascension-Mysteries-Revealing-Cosmic-Between-ebook/dp/B0191ZL2EC

Acknowledgments

My deepest gratitude and appreciation go to my editor, Marigold, who gave me invaluable help with her outstanding editing skills and powerful insight into the subject of the book. I also give profound thanks to a few dear people in my life who took the time to read certain chapters as I wrote them and gave their feedback: Bob Basham, Deborah Morris, Lauren Matthews, and Pat Basham. All of what they told me helped me to steer my way through disturbing material and to present it in the most positive and effective way possible.

Vidya Frazier has studied spiritual teachings from both western and eastern traditions for over 40 years. In 1993, she felt called to India to visit the spiritual master Papaji. Upon returning, she wrote *The Art of Letting Go: A Pathway to Inner Freedom* and began offering individual sessions, groups and workshops based on this book.

In 2007, she was invited to attend the Oneness University in India and was initiated as a Oneness Blessing Facilitator. She returned and offered the blessing to hundreds of people. Since then, she has studied with quantum healer Dell Morris and author Jim Self.

In 2014, Vidya published her first book on the theme of Ascension, *Awakening to the Fifth Dimension—A Guide for Navigating the Global Shift* and has given a number of presentations and interviews on the subject. A year later, she published a second book, a more in-depth exploration on the same theme: *Ascension: Embracing the Transformation.*

Currently offering sessions of Ascension counseling and Quantum Healing, Vidya assists people to find their way with clarity and ease through the powerful energies of the Shift of consciousness that is now occurring across the planet. She also assists people in discovering their spiritual purpose in life and stepping more fully into expressing it.

Drawing on forty years as a licensed psychotherapist, hypnotherapist, and spiritual guide, as well as on her own spiritual awakening experiences, Vidya serves as a unique bridge between the worlds of psychology and spiritual awakening.

Contact Vidya at www.vidyafrazier.com.

CPSIA information can be obtained
at www.ICGtesting.com
Printed in the USA
BVOW08s0923230318
511307BV00001B/255/P